# C A T H O L I C
# HOUSEHOLD
# BLESSINGS
# & PRAYERS

Bishops' Committee on the Liturgy
National Conference of Catholic Bishops

In its planning document, as approved by the general membership of the National Conference of Catholic Bishops in November 1987, the Bishops' Committee on the Liturgy was authorized to prepare a book of prayers and blessings for use by Catholic families and households. *Catholic Household Blessings and Prayers* was approved by the NCCB Administrative Committee in March 1988 and is authorized for publication by the undersigned.

Monsignor Daniel F. Hoye
General Secretary
May 10, 1988                                                                            NCCB/USCC

ISBN 1-55586-220-9

# Table of Contents

**PART III: TIMES IN LIFE: BLESSINGS OF
FAMILY MEMBERS**

## PART IV: BLESSINGS FOR VARIOUS TIMES AND PLACES

# FOREWORD

Since the promulgation of the *Constitution on the Sacred Liturgy* of the Second Vatican Council, all of us have experienced the first steps toward a renewal of the liturgy of the Church. We see clearly now that this liturgical renewal cannot be a matter of texts and rubrics only; the heart of this renewal is prayer. And the key to renewing the prayer of the Sunday assembly is enkindling a love for and practice of prayer in the hearts of those who make up the Church. Prayer must happen in the "little churches"—the households, the families—if the Sunday assembly is to become a community of prayer. The Council taught that the liturgy "is the primary and indispensable source from which the faithful are to derive the true Christian spirit"

(*Constitution on the Sacred Liturgy,* 14). How can that spirit come to fill and give shape to our lives unless it is there in the prayers of individuals and families?

In 1984, a *Book of Blessings* was published by the Vatican Congregation for Divine Worship. It includes many texts for blessings that are to be used by both clergy and laity and suggests that the local Church adapt and expand these rites. We have accepted this invitation to provide a book of blessings and prayers for all Catholics in the United States. In doing so, we have sought ways in which our Church's liturgy can become a strong and constant source of the "true Christian spirit" for clergy and laity alike.

And so, this book is devoted to that "bond of prayer" that joins the prayer of the Sunday assembly to the daily prayers of every Catholic, the bond between Roman Catholics of all descriptions, and our bond to other Christians and, in many ways, to Jews from whom we have learned so much of our prayer.

We hope that this book will find a place in every Catholic household—but not a place to rest. This book and the family's Bible, side by side, should become worn out with use. Along with other signs— the cross, holy water, blessed candles—the presence of the Bible and this book of prayers expresses a way of life. This Catholic way—a way of daily justice, of service, and of care that is found around the family table and around the world's wide table— is our baptismal charge. It is the garment we put on at baptism; we are clothed with Christ.

From one generation to the next, we must learn, hold dear, and hand on the words and gestures, the songs and Scriptures of our faith. At the altar on Sunday, at table and at bedside all week, we learn throughout our lives who we are: the Body of Christ.

We address a special word to parents. Some of you grew up with such words and ways of prayer. Some did not. All of us, whatever our background, are still learning to pray, still learning to be Christians. Take this book, then, and search through it. Learn well, for your own sake, some of its daily prayers, some of its blessings for ordinary and special times. Begin to pray beside your children even when they are very young. Pray in your own words, by all means, but pray especially the words of the Church. Pray because you yourself need to pray. Then, as your children grow, invite them into this prayer. Bless them each night. Pray at table with them each evening. Let them hear you singing the songs of faith and reading the holy Scriptures. Let them know that fasting and almsgiving, care for the poor and the sick, and daily intercession for justice and for peace are what you hold most dear.

To all Catholics we say: take time with these pages. Come to know the strength of the texts they hold. Find those prayers and rites that can be celebrated in your life and in your home. Wear this book out with use until you know much of it by heart.

Let us bless the Lord!

Bishops' Committee on the Liturgy
National Conference of Catholic Bishops
Solemnity of Pentecost
May 22, 1988

# INTRODUCTION

## HOW TO USE THIS BOOK

Can the prayers and the rites of a people be put into a book?

The first and last answer is no. Prayers and rites exist not on paper but in life. This is most true when we speak of the prayers and rites that belong to everyone. The sign of the cross is not learned from a book but from a parent.

Roman Catholics, like any people who share a faith and a way of life, need the words and gestures that express that faith and teach that way of life. These are the simple prayers at table and bedside, the ways of keeping Lent, and the blessings in sickness and at the time of death. Such things belong in books only as a help to bring them to life. In our time, we have had to learn again how hard it is and yet how essential that prayer and rite belong to all the baptized.

This book has been assembled to help Catholics in the United States remember or learn anew. It contains the prayers and rites of the baptized. It is meant to do all that a book can do to remind us of our words, our texts. Most of these have marked the days and nights, births and deaths of scores of generations. Some are newer expressions of the same faith. The book is not simply a random collection of prayers, however. It is an "order" of prayer, an ordering of this treasure of ours. It is offered so that all the baptized—whatever else their involvement may be as church members—may have access to their heritage and may come to know the prayers that are both their duty and their privilege.

The two decades since the Second Vatican Council have seen the beginning of renewal in the various public rites of the Church. Above all else, this renewal is directed toward the full, active, and conscious participation of all the baptized. To a great extent, that goal must wait until the people who assemble for the Sunday liturgy are people who know their part well, know it truly by heart, and know it because they know what it is to praise God, to attend to the Scriptures, to intercede, and to give thanks.

These are the ordinary ways learned day by day, season by season. They are learned at home, learned alone, or learned as part of a family. They are not luxuries, pieties for the few, but are the fibers that bind a baptized person to Church, to Christ, and to each other. Without them, we drift. Without them, the notion of being a Church is lost to us. In the time and culture where we live, that is a very real danger.

The word *household* appears in the title of this book. It could have been *family*, but the intention here is to provide a book for every Catholic. Some of the rites in this book will be appropriate only in a setting where several live together, but much is meant also for the individual Catholic. In every case, this book is to be an order of prayer, a way of reminding, and a way of learning what belongs to us. For all—certainly parents, but all who make up the Church—these prayers and rites are something we take with reverence for all the generations that have shaped them for us. We will give something of ourselves to these prayers, something that they yet lack, something that can form Christians in our time and place. Then we will hand them on for they are not finally ours. They belong to this communion of saints in which we walk and in which our children and their children may also walk.

## CONTENT OF THIS BOOK

The heart of this book is "The Daily Blessings." Here are the words for the various moments of morning, daytime, evening, and nighttime. Many of them you already know by heart; others you will recognize. Except for the seasonal blessings at table, these are prayers for every day, year in and year out. In "The Daily Blessings," the first page of each section contains the few and always brief prayers that are commended to you for memorization, for learning "by heart." On the following page or pages are other texts—longer, perhaps less familiar, but which are also suitable for learning by heart. It is not intended that this book be opened at the various times mentioned in "The Daily Blessings." Rather, the book is to be put aside as the prayers are memorized. These prayers cannot live except in our hearts.

It is hoped that this book will have its permanent place beside the table where the evening meal is taken, there to be opened to familiar pages each day. Many of the blessings in the other parts of the book, blessings that may be used only once a year or even less frequently, will find their best "home" at the evening meal of the family.

The Table of Contents is an important tool for those who want to make good use of all that follows "The Daily Blessings." Turn to it as you read through the overview here.

Part II is called "Days and Seasons." The Introduction presents a description of the church year. This is followed by prayers for keeping the Lord's Day which, before all else, is the way Christians mark their days. Blessings and prayers follow for Advent and Christmastime, for Lent and for Eastertime. Days of special observance are then noted: saints' days, fast days, and national days.

Part III, "Times in Life: Blessings of Family Members," begins with a simple blessing of the family and continues with prayers and blessings to mark the life cycle: birth and adoption, child rearing, marriage, sickness, and death. For each of these, many different moments are marked with brief prayers or longer rites.

In Part IV, "Blessings for Various Times and Places," are the blessings associated with comings and goings: guests, a child moving away, leaving a home, or coming to a new home. Here also are blessings for places of work, texts for times of special joy or difficulty, and a general form of blessing.

The final section, "Common Prayers," contains texts that are familiar or especially beautiful, which are not used in the previous part of the book. They are presented here either by the type of prayer (for example, prayers of intercession, litanies, psalms) or by the subject (for example, prayers addressed to the Blessed Virgin Mary). Prayers in other languages that remain part of our Catholic heritage are given and explained here. The final sections of Part V contain a fuller form of Morning Prayer and Evening Prayer taken from the Church's Liturgy of the Hours.

The Appendix to the book presents the Church's calendar of saints' days.

## USING THE PRAYERS AND BLESSINGS

Except for the table prayers, "The Daily Blessings" of Part I will usually be used by an individual alone or by a parent and child. No special notes are necessary to explain their use.

The table blessings of Part I, and the longer rites that fill much of the rest of the book, suggest a very simple order. It is an order that we know something about from Sunday Mass, an order that should be as much at home within the family as it is with the larger assembly on Sunday.

These rites presume a leader, a person who becomes familiar with the rite by reading its words beforehand, by making any preparations necessary (for example, asking someone else to prepare the scripture reading), and by preparing with prayer to be a leader of prayer. Above all, this leader must be one who sees that our rites are more than directions and readings in books. They are simply this: what we Catholics do, what we are learning to do, that we might express for some moment (be it the blessing of a Christmas tree or the death of a grandparent) what our baptized lives are about. God's word and the intercession and the thanksgiving thus come to be ours.

The leader generally should be the appropriate person: someone able to lead well, someone who can give the prayer dignity. Such dignity comes from how well the leader knows the place of prayer in a Christian's life. In most families, the leader will not always be the same person.

Anyone who is to lead should be familiar with the structure of the rites that is most commonly found here. This order is not unlike that of the Mass. At Mass, we gather and are called to prayer together; we listen to the Scriptures and homily and join in prayers of intercession; then we give God thanks and praise over the bread and wine which, as the Body and Blood of Christ, we share in holy communion; finally we take leave of one another.

In these rites of blessing, most of these elements are found:

- *Gathering and Call to Prayer:* the sign of the cross, the leader's initial words, and, sometimes, the leader's words of introduction.

- *The Reading of Scripture:* a short text that is read from the family's Bible, followed by a few moments of reflection.

- *Prayers of Intercession:* anyone present may speak prayers for the needs of the world as well as for the particular needs of the family; usually this is concluded with the Lord's Prayer.

- *Prayer of Blessing:* a prayer that praises God and invokes God's blessing in the circumstances that have occasioned the rite.

- *Conclusion:* the sign of the cross and a final word of praise. Often, all then join in song.

The leader and all members of the household need to make this their own. A book of rites is, to some extent, like a book of recipes. The contents and the order of doing things are important, but they also need to become the possession of those who do them. So a household, respecting the tradition, still needs to let that tradition live and grow in its midst.

All of this will happen gradually. To help with this, some notes follow about particular elements in these prayers. They are intended to help those who use this book to be at home in its pages.

*Words of address and response.* "The Lord be with you." "This is the Word of the Lord." "Blessed be God for ever." "Let us bless the Lord." Throughout these rites, there are words between leader and other participants, words that all know by heart. In a sense, these are the most crucial prayers we have, tiny little greetings and acclamations that gather up the whole of a Christian's life. There are not many of these used in this book, and most are already familiar. A few of them may be new, and this should be foreseen so that the words can be taught. The leader's part in these exchanges should always be spoken carefully, without rushing.

*The readings of Scripture.* The Scripture text should always be prepared ahead of time. Usually, it is done by someone other than the leader. Though many Scripture texts are provided within this book, it would be better to use the family's Bible for all scripture readings. This should be a book that is treated with reverence. It should be a good translation of the Scriptures. In many cases, it might also be a book where the family keeps a record of births, baptism, deaths, and other significant events. Often, the rites will suggest alternative Scripture readings. The leader should go over these beforehand to select the one that is most appropriate. After the reader says, "This is the Word of the Lord," and all respond, "Thanks be to God," a few long moments of silence will allow for reflection on the words that have been heard. This silence should simply be everyone's expectation.

*Prayers of intercession.* Since the "Prayer of the Faithful" has been restored to Sunday Mass, Catholics are coming to understand how this way of praying is to be part of our lives. To be baptized is to be made responsible for interceding, for holding in one's heart all the sorrows and joys and needs of the world, and lifting these to the Lord in daily prayer. It is a task of remembering, of living one's life with eyes wide open to the things God would have us care about. And it is calling on God to remember, to listen, to come to our assistance. Within these rites, the words of such intercession are not written out. Usually, it is only noted that people are to speak their prayers for large and small needs. Sometimes, the ancient forms of "Let us pray to the Lord: Lord, hear our prayer," or "Lord, have mercy," can be used to conclude each intercession. These prayers should always be unhurried. Some of the beautiful forms that tradition has given to the intercession will be found in Part V, nos. 1-4. Those examples should be used on occasion to show us how intercessions always balance the needs of the wider world with those of the household. Most often, the Lord's Prayer will serve to conclude the intercessions as it asks for God's will to be done, for our daily bread, and for forgiveness.

*Prayers of blessing and other prayers.* These are prayers spoken by the leader, including the central prayer of blessing in each rite. Usually, these prayers first address God and speak of some deed of God, then ask God's blessing on this particular person or persons in this special moment. Some of these prayers are ancient texts; others are contemporary. This will be seen in their images and language. All of them belong to the Church and deserve the careful preparation and proclamation by the leader. In some cases, they are preceded by the invitation, "Let us pray," and a time of silence so that thoughts may be gathered and focused before the prayer itself is spoken. At the end, the "Amen" of all those present is an affirmation of what the leader has spoken.

*Posture.* Whether people stand or sit or kneel will usually depend on the place of the blessing and other circumstances. In general, participants should be seated for listening to Scripture and for silent reflection and should stand during the beginning of the rite and for all that follows the Scripture. Kneeling may be appropriate at some parts of some rites. A few rites call for walking or processing. Like other elements, this matter of posture should become second nature. It should not be necessary to call out directions; familiarity with the rites will bring an ease with standing and sitting. In general, Christians sit for listening and for reflection, stand to pray their intercession and praise, and kneel in penance or adoration.

*Gesture.* Sometimes specific gestures are suggested within the rites: placing hands on the person being blessed or joining hands for the Lord's Prayer. Such gestures should also become second nature, very natural practices within the household. Other gestures may also acquire such a natural place, for example, hands folded during prayers of intercessions or hands held out and open during prayers of praise and thanksgiving. Other gestures relate to objects used in blessing, for example, the lighting of a candle at table prayer (in the evening in a family, this may be a task given to a child). Like all gestures, it should be done with reverence and care.

*Silence.* Silence gives a pace and a reverence to our prayer. It is particularly important after the reading of Scripture. Silence should be long enough for the attention to focus and for everyone to be at ease within the silence. Children are often better at keeping such a silence than most adults would imagine.

*Song.* Prayer together—by any group of any faith—almost always means chanting and singing. The meanings of our prayer are too great to be contained by the speaking voice, and the unity that song embodies strengthens the community. The rites in this book usually suggest song at the conclusion of a rite. The hymns given will be known to a great number of Catholics. Though many people are not yet comfortable with singing at times of family prayer, it is important to attempt at least very simple pieces. Ideally, the singing of a single verse would be a part of daily prayer at table together.

Through such songs, known by heart, we learn prayer in a new and broader way. Even when a person prays alone, the melodies of our hymns provide a way to recall and ponder the mysteries of our faith. When children grow up in a home where there is song within their prayer, they bring this gift to their parish community. Sometimes, then, it may be possible to expand the place of song in these prayers, for example, by singing a psalm after a scripture reading, or by repeating a simple refrain or acclamation.

*Psalms.* Psalms are found in Part I and Part V and, occasionally, in the other rites. In itself, this does not express the great importance of the Psalms to our prayer. These songs come to us from the Hebrew Scripture; they have been basic to Jewish prayer since before the time of Jesus. They were the prayers of Jesus. They have been the prayers of the Church in public and in private. It is from the Psalms that we can learn to pray. Adults should strive to learn short psalms or portions of psalms by heart. Parents and children can learn together Psalm 23, Psalm 121, Psalm 130, and others that fit into our daily or seasonal prayer.

## A BLESSING

For Jews and for Christians, the notion of blessing is bound up with praising God and giving thanks to God; bound up with our way of seeing, understanding, and being in this world and in the human community. The prayer of blessing is part of our heritage from Judaism, and it continues to be a living part of Jewish life today. This lasting bond between Jews and Christians is often expressed in this book by the use of texts that come from the Jewish tradition.

## CONCLUSION

Whether we say simply, "God bless you," or join in a rite of song and prayer and Scripture, we are proclaiming the good news of God's love and reign.

# PART I
# THE DAILY BLESSINGS

# THE CHURCH'S PRAYER

The Lord's Prayer, either sung or recited by one person alone or by many assembled, is the foundation of the Church's daily prayer. In these words from Matthew, chapter 6, the baptized people bless the Lord's name and pray for God's kingdom, for daily bread, and for forgiveness. Even when no other prayers can be prayed, this one is commended to each Christian to be used in the morning, during the day, and at night. The first translation is that commonly used by Roman Catholics. The second is a translation now shared by Catholics and many other English-speaking Christians. The third text is the shorter version of the Lord's Prayer found in the gospel of Luke (11:2-4).

Our Father, who art in heaven,
hallowed be thy name;
thy kingdom come;
thy will be done on earth as it is in
    heaven.
Give us this day our daily bread;
and forgive us our trespasses
as we forgive those who trespass
    against us;
and lead us not into temptation,
but deliver us from evil.
Amen.

Our Father in heaven,
  hallowed be your name,
  your kingdom come,
  your will be done,
  on earth as in heaven.
Give us today our daily bread.
Forgive us our sins
  as we forgive those who sin against us.
Save us from the time of trial
  and deliver us from evil.
For the kingdom, the power, and the glory are
  yours,
  now and for ever.
Amen.


Father, hallowed be your name,
  your kingdom come.
  Give us each day our daily bread
  and forgive us our sins,
  for we ourselves forgive everyone in debt to
  us,
  and do not subject us to the final test.

# WAKING

*Upon waking, make the sign of the cross and say:*

In the name of the Father, and of the Son, and of the Holy Spirit. Amen.

*Or trace a small cross on the lips and say:*

Lord, open my lips,
and my mouth will proclaim your praise.

## FOR EVERY DAY

Glory to the Father, and to the Son, and to the
  Holy Spirit:
as it was in the beginning, is now, and will be for
  ever.
(Amen.)

*Gloria Patri*


Holy, holy, holy Lord, God of power and might,
heaven and earth are full of your glory.
Hosanna in the highest.

*Sanctus*


Hear, O Israel!
The Lord is our God, the Lord alone!
Blessed is God's glorious kingdom for ever and
  ever.
You shall love the Lord, your God, with all your
  mind,
and with all your soul, and with all your
  strength.

*Sh'ma Israel*

## FOR SUNDAY

Glory to God in the highest,
   and peace to his people on earth.

Lord God, heavenly King,
almighty God and Father,
   we worship you, we give you thanks,
   we praise you for your glory.

Lord Jesus Christ, only Son of the Father,
Lord God, Lamb of God,
you take away the sin of the world:
   have mercy on us;
you are seated at the right hand of the Father:
   receive our prayer.
For you alone are the Holy One,
you alone are the Lord,
you alone are the Most High,
   Jesus Christ,
   with the Holy Spirit,
   in the glory of God the Father. Amen.

*Gloria in excelsis Deo*

## WHEN OPENING THE EYES

Blessed are you, Lord, God of all creation:
you open the eyes of the blind.

## WHEN RISING

Blessed are you, Lord, God of all creation:
you raise up those who are bowed down.

Blessed are you, Lord, God of all creation:
you set captives free.


Awake, O sleeper,
and arise from the dead,
and Christ will give you light.

Ephesians 5:14


I arise today
through God's strength to pilot me,
God's might to uphold me,
God's wisdom to guide me,
God's eye to look before me,
God's ear to hear me,
God's hand to guard me,
God's way to lie before me,
God's shield to protect me,
God's hosts to save me from the snares of the
    devil.

*Saint Patrick's Breastplate*

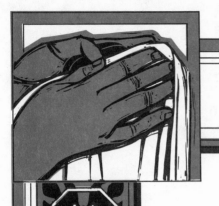

# WASHING AND DRESSING

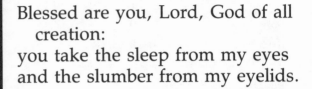

Blessed are you, Lord, God of all
  creation:
you take the sleep from my eyes
and the slumber from my eyelids.

Blessed are you, Lord, God of all
  creation:
you clothe the naked.

Bless, O Christ, my face.
Let my face bless everything.
Bless, O Christ, my eyes.
Let my eyes bless all they see.

Blessed are you, Lord, God of all
  creation:
you formed us in wisdom
and gave us the paths and
  openings in our bodies.

## FOR LENT

Have mercy on me, O God, in your goodness;
   in the greatness of your compassion wipe out
   my offense.
Thoroughly wash me from my guilt
   and of my sin cleanse me.

Let me'hear the sounds of joy and gladness;
   the bones you have crushed shall rejoice.
Turn away your face from my sins,
   and blot out all my guilt.

A clean heart create for me, O God,
   and a steadfast spirit renew within me.
Cast me not out from your presence,
   and your holy spirit take not from me.

Psalm 51:3-4,10-13 (Miserere)

## FOR EASTERTIME AND SUNDAYS

Give thanks to the LORD, for he is good,
   for his mercy endures forever.

I was hard pressed and was falling,
   but the LORD helped me.
My strength and my courage is the LORD,
   and he has been my savior.

You are my God, and I give thanks to you;
   O my God, I extol you.
Give thanks to the LORD, for he is good;
   for his kindness endures forever.

Psalm 118:1,13-14,28-29


## FOR ALL OTHER DAYS

*The Benedictus (Canticle of Zechariah) is an
ancient morning prayer. It is customary to make
the sign of the cross during the first words.*

+ Blessed be the Lord, the God of Israel;
he has come to his people and set them free.

He has raised up for us a mighty savior,
born of the house of his servant David.

Through his holy prophets he promised of old,
   that he would save us from our enemies,
   from the hands of all who hate us.

He promised to show mercy to our fathers
and to remember his holy covenant.

This was the oath he swore to our father
   Abraham:

to set us free from the hands of our enemies,
free to worship him without fear
holy and righteous in his sight all the days of our
    life.

You, my child, shall be called the prophet of the
    Most High
for you will go before the Lord to prepare his
    way,

to give his people knowledge of salvation
by the forgiveness of their sins.

In the tender compassion of our God
the dawn from on high shall break upon us,
to shine on those who dwell in darkness
    and the shadow of death,
and to guide our feet into the way of peace.

Luke 1:68-79 (*Benedictus*)

# GOING OUT FROM HOME EACH DAY

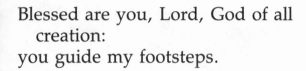

Blessed are you, Lord, God of all
    creation:
you guide my footsteps.


Blessed are you, Lord, God of all
    creation:
you spread out the earth upon the
    waters.

Direct our steps to yourself, O God,
and show us how to walk in charity and peace.


Praise the LORD from the heavens,
   praise him in the heights;
Praise him, all you his angels,
   praise him, all you his hosts.
Praise him, sun and moon;
   praise him, all you shining stars.
Praise him, you highest heavens,
   and you waters above the heavens.
Let them praise the name of the LORD,
   for he commanded and they were created;
He established them forever and ever;
   he gave them a duty which shall not pass
   away.


Praise the LORD from the earth,
   you sea monsters and all depths;
Fire and hail, snow and mist,
   storm winds that fulfill his word;
You mountains and all you hills,
   you fruit trees and all you cedars;
You wild beasts and all tame animals,
   you creeping things and you winged fowl.

Let the kings of earth and all peoples,
　　the princes and all the judges of the earth,
Young men too, and maidens,
　　old men and boys,
Praise the name of the LORD,
　　for his name alone is exalted;
His majesty is above earth and heaven,
　　and he has lifted up the horn of his people.
Be this his praise from all his faithful ones,
　　from the children of Israel, the people
　　　close to him.   Alleluia.

Psalm 148


Come, let us sing joyfully to the LORD;
　　let us acclaim the Rock of our salvation.
Let us greet him with thanksgiving;
　　let us joyfully sing psalms to him.
For the LORD is a great God,
　　and a great king above all gods;
In his hands are the depths of the earth,
　　and the tops of the mountains are his.
His is the sea, for he has made it,
　　and the dry land, which his hands have
　　　formed.

Come, let us bow down in worship;
　　let us kneel before the LORD who made us.
For he is our God,
　　and we are the people he shepherds,
　　　the flock he guides.

Psalm 95:1-7

## FOR THE DAY'S WORK AT HOME

God be in my head, and in my understanding;
God be in my eyes, and in my looking;
God be in my mouth, and in my speaking;
God be in my heart, and in my thinking;
God be at my end, and at my departing.

# AT NOON

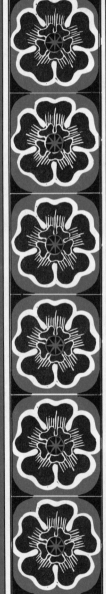

V. The angel spoke God's message to Mary,
R. and she conceived of the Holy Spirit.
Hail, Mary. . . .

V. "I am the lowly servant of the Lord:
R. let it be done to me according to your word."
Hail, Mary. . . .

V. And the Word became flesh
R. and lived among us.
Hail, Mary. . . .

V. Pray for us, holy Mother of God,
R. that we may become worthy of the promises of Christ.

Let us pray.

Lord,
fill our hearts with your grace:
once, through the message of an angel
you revealed to us the incarnation of your
   Son;
now, through his suffering and death
lead us to the glory of his resurrection.

We ask this through Christ our Lord.
R. Amen.

*The Angelus*

*This is also prayed in the early morning and at
evening.*

*The Hail Mary is an ancient prayer whose first
verses come from Luke's gospel, the words of the
angel and the words of Elizabeth. The final lines
invoke Mary's protection in the present moment
and at the time of death.*

Hail Mary, full of grace,
the Lord is with you!
Blessed are you among women,
and blessed is the fruit of your womb, Jesus.
Holy Mary, Mother of God,
pray for us sinners,
now and at the hour of our death.
Amen.

# TAKING FOOD AND DRINK

**BEFORE EATING AND DRINKING**

Bless + us, O Lord, and these
    your gifts
which we are about to receive from
    your goodness.
Through Christ our Lord.
R. Amen.


**AFTER EATING AND DRINKING**

We give you thanks for all your
    gifts, almighty God,
living and reigning now and for
    ever.
R. Amen.

Blessed are you, Lord, God of all creation:
you bring forth bread from the earth.

God is blessed in all his gifts
and holy in all his works,
who lives and reigns for ever and ever.
R. Amen.

All the world hopes in you, O Lord,
that you will give us food in our hunger.
You open wide your hand
and we are filled with good things.

Cf. Psalm 104

Blessed be the Lord,
of whose bounty we have received
and by whose goodness we live.

The poor shall eat and shall have their fill.
Those who long for the Lord shall give him
    praise.
May their hearts live for ever.

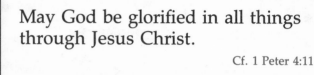

# LABOR, SERVICE, STUDY, AND ALMSGIVING

May God be glorified in all things through Jesus Christ.

Cf. 1 Peter 4:11

May the peace of God that is
  beyond all understanding
guard our hearts and our thoughts
  in Christ Jesus.

Cf. Philippians 4:7

We give you thanks, our Father!
You call us to share the lot of the saints in light!

Cf. Colossians 1:12

## IN DEEDS OF SERVICE

In all our words and actions
let us give thanks to God
in the name of the Lord Jesus.

Cf. Colossians 3:17

May God put our faith into action,
to work in love, to persevere in hope,
through our Lord Jesus Christ.

Cf. 1 Thessalonians 1:3

## WHEN GIVING OR RECEIVING ALMS

May God fully supply all our needs
according to his generosity, with magnificence,
in Christ Jesus!
To God be glory for ever and ever!

Cf. Philippians 4:19-20

Blessed are you, Lord, God of tenderness and
    compassion,
rich in kindness and faithfulness.

Cf. Exodus 34:6


God of the humble and help of the oppressed:
Blessed are you, Lord!
Support of the weak and refuge of the forsaken:
Blessed are you, Lord!

Cf. Judith 9:11


## AT WORK

Day by day we bless you, Lord.
We praise your name for ever.


Jesus, gentle and humble of heart, have mercy
    on us.
Mary, mirror of justice, pray for us.
Joseph, model of workers, pray for us.


May we know the shortness of our days,
that we may learn wisdom.

Lord,
may everything we do
begin with your inspiration
and continue with your help
so that all our prayers and works
may begin in you
and by you be happily ended.

We ask this through Christ our Lord.
R. Amen.


## AT STUDY

Teach me to do your will, for you are my God.
Psalm 143:10


[May] we grow in grace and in the knowledge
of our Lord and savior Jesus Christ.
To him be glory now and to the day of eternity
2 Peter 3:18

# COMING HOME
# EACH DAY

Hear us, Lord,
and send your angel from heaven
to visit and protect,
to comfort and defend
all who live in this house.

May the Lord of peace give us
    peace
all the time and in every way.
The Lord be with us.

Cf. 2 Thessalonians 3:16

O radiant Light, O Sun divine,
Of God the Father's deathless face,
O Image of the light sublime
That fills the heav'nly dwelling
    place.

Lord Jesus Christ, as daylight
    fades,

As shine the lights of eventide,
We praise the Father with the Son,
The Spirit blest and with them one.

O Son of God, the source of life,
Praise is your due by night and day;
Our [untarnished] lips must raise the
   strain
Of your proclaimed and splendid name.

Ancient Greek Hymn for Evening: "Phos Hilaron"

## FOR EVENING DURING LENT

Truly you have formed my inmost being;
   you knit me in my mother's womb.
I give you thanks that I am fearfully, wonderfully
   made;
   wonderful are your works.

Probe me, O God, and know my heart;
   try me, and know my thoughts;
See if my way is crooked,
   and lead me in the way of old.

Psalm 139:13-14,23-24

## FOR EVENING ON SUNDAY AND DURING EASTERTIME

Alleluia! Praise the Lord, all you nations;
glorify him, all you peoples!
For steadfast in his kindness toward us,
and the fidelity of the Lord endures forever.

Psalm 117

## ON ALL OTHER DAYS

*The Magnificat (Canticle of Mary) is an ancient
evening prayer. It is customary to make the sign
of the cross during the first words.*

+ My soul proclaims the greatness of the Lord,
my spirit rejoices in God my Savior;
for he has looked with favor on his lowly
    servant.

From this day all generations will call me blessed:
the Almighty has done great things for me,
and holy is his Name.

He has mercy on those who fear him
in every generation.

He has shown the strength of his arm,
he has scattered the proud in their conceit.

He has cast down the mighty from their thrones,
and has lifted up the lowly.

He has filled the hungry with good things,
and the rich he has sent away empty.

He has come to the help of his servant Israel
for he has remembered his promise of mercy,
the promise he made to our fathers,
to Abraham and his children for ever.

Luke 1:46-55 (*Magnificat*)

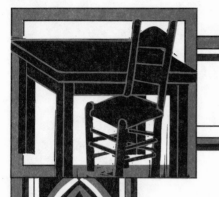

# AT TABLE

*When all are seated, begin with the sign of the cross:*

In the name of the Father, and of the Son, and of the Holy Spirit. Amen.

*If several pray together, they may alternate the verses:*

[The eyes of all creatures] look to
   you to give them food in
      due time.
When you give it to them, they
   gather it;
   when you open your hand,
   they are filled with good things.

Psalm 104:27-28

*The leader says:*

Let us call on the name of the Father,
who always takes care of his children.

*All pray together:*

Our Father. . . .

For the kingdom, the power, and the
    glory are yours,
now and for ever.

Bless + us, O Lord, and these your gifts
which we are about to receive from your
    goodness.
Through Christ our Lord.
R. Amen.

> *One of the following prayers may be used instead
> of "The eyes of all creatures look to you":*

Lord, the lover of life,
you feed the birds of the skies
and array the lilies of the field.
We bless you for all your creatures
and for the food we are about to receive.
We humbly pray that in your goodness
you will provide for our brothers and sisters
who are hungry.

We ask this through Christ our Lord.
R. Amen.

Blessed are you, almighty Father,
who give us our daily bread.
Blessed is your only begotten Son,
who continually feeds us on the word of life.
Blessed is the Holy Spirit,
who brings us together at this table of love.
Blessed be God now and for ever.
R. Amen.

*Bread may be lifted up and broken:*

Blessed are you, Lord, God of all creation:
you bring forth bread from the earth.
Blessed be God for ever.

*All respond:*

Blessed be God for ever.

*A cup of wine may be lifted up:*

Blessed are you, Lord, God all creation:
creator of the fruit of the vine.
Blessed be God for ever.

*All respond:*

Blessed be God for ever.

*This blessing may be sung to any appropriate tune such as "The Old Hundreth" (Praise God from Whom All Blessings Flow):*

Be present at our table, Lord.
Be here and everywhere adored.
Thy creatures bless and grant that we
may feast in Paradise with thee.

*One of the following prayers may be used instead of "Bless us, O Lord":*

Lord, our God,
with fatherly love you come to the aid of your
    children.
Bless us and these your gifts
which we are about to receive from your
    goodness.
Grant that all peoples may be gladdened
by the favors of your providence.

We ask this through Christ our Lord.
R. Amen.


God of all goodness,
through the breaking of bread together
you strengthen the bonds that unite us in love.
Bless + us and these your gifts.
Grant that as we sit down together at table
in joy and sincerity,
we may grow always closer in the bonds of love.

We ask this through Christ our Lord.
R. Amen.

May your gifts refresh us, O Lord,
and your grace give us strength.
R. Amen.

# THANKSGIVING AFTER MEALS

Let all your works praise you,
   O Lord.
Let all your people bless you.

*All pray together:*

We give you thanks for all your
   gifts, almighty God,
living and reigning now and for
   ever.
R. Amen.

For the sake of your name,
   O Lord,
reward those who have been good
   to us
and give them eternal life.
R. Amen.

Or:

Lord, give all people the food they need,
so that they may join us in giving you
thanks.
R. Amen.

*When members of the household are absent, the
leader concludes:*

May God be with us
and with N. (and N.)
R. Amen.

*One or more of these prayers may be used instead:*

*The leader says:*

Blessed be the name of the Lord.

*All respond:*

Now and forever.

We thank you, O Lord, the giver of all good
   gifts,
who have kindly brought us together at this
   table.
Refreshed in body, may we make our earthly
   journey in joy
and one day arrive at the banquet table of
   heaven.

We ask this through Christ our Lord.
R. Amen.


We thank you, our God,
for the food you have given us.
Make our sharing this bread together
lead to a renewal of our communion with you,
with one another, and with all creatures.

We ask this through Christ our Lord.
R. Amen.


Lord, you feed every living thing.
We have eaten together at this table; keep us in
   your love.
Give us true concern for the least of our sisters
   and brothers,
so that as we gladly share our food with them,
we may also sit down together with them
at the table of the kingdom of heaven.

We ask this through Christ our Lord.
R. Amen.

Lord, you have fed us from your gifts and favors;
fill us with your mercy,
for you live and reign for ever and ever.
R. Amen.

God is blessed in all his gifts
and holy in all his works,
who lives and reigns for ever and ever.
R. Amen.

# AT TABLE ON SUNDAY

*One person lights a candle and says:*

Jesus Christ is the light of the world.

*All respond:*

A light no darkness can overpower.

*The leader lifts up the bread and prays:*

We thank you, Father,
for the life and knowledge you
    have revealed to us
through your child Jesus.
Glory be yours through all ages.
As grain once scattered on the
    hillside
was in this broken bread made
    one,
so from all lands may we be
    gathered
into your kingdom by your Son.

*The Didache*

*All respond "Amen" to each blessing; parents may place their hands on their children as they bless them:*

The Lord bless us and keep us.
R. Amen.
The Lord's face shine upon us and be
   gracious to us.
R. Amen.
The Lord look upon us with kindness and
   give us peace.
R. Amen.

*Then an acclamation or song may be sung.*

Praise God from whom all blessings flow.
Praise God all creatures here below.
Praise God above, ye heavenly host.
Praise Father, Son and Holy Ghost.

# AT TABLE
# ON DAYS OF FASTING
# AND ALMSGIVING

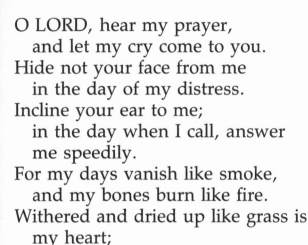

O LORD, hear my prayer,
  and let my cry come to you.
Hide not your face from me
  in the day of my distress.
Incline your ear to me;
  in the day when I call, answer
  me speedily.
For my days vanish like smoke,
  and my bones burn like fire.
Withered and dried up like grass is
  my heart;
  I forget to eat my bread.

I am sleepless, and I moan;
  I am like a sparrow alone on the
  housetop.

For I eat ashes like bread
  and mingle my drink with tears.

My days are like a lengthening shadow,
    and I wither like grass.
But you, O LORD, abide forever,
    and your name through all generations.

Psalm 102:2-5,8,10,12-13

## ON FRIDAYS

All praise be yours, God our Creator,
as we wait in joyful hope
for the flowering of justice
and the fullness of peace.
All praise for this day, this Friday.
By our weekly fasting and prayer,
cast out the spirit of war, of fear and mistrust,
and make us grow hungry for human kindness,
thirsty for solidarity with all the people of your
    dear earth.
May all our prayer, our fasting, and our deeds
be done in the name of Jesus.
R. Amen.

# AT TABLE DURING ADVENT

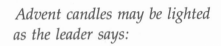

*Advent candles may be lighted
as the leader says:*

Blessed are you, Lord, God
 of all creation:
in the darkness and in the light.

Blessed are you
in this food and in our sharing.

Blessed are you as we wait
 in joyful hope
for the coming of our savior,
 Jesus Christ.

*All respond:*

For the kingdom, the power, and the
glory are yours, now and for ever.

*The leader says:*

Come, Lord Jesus!

*All respond:*

Come quickly!

*Another form of Advent prayer begins with the sign of the cross.*

In the name of the Father, and of the Son, and of the Holy Spirit. Amen.

*Someone at table reads one of the following Scriptures or the Scripture assigned to the liturgy of the day.*

**A** Listen to the words of the prophet Isaiah:

Trust in the LORD forever!
    For the LORD is an eternal Rock.
He humbles those in high places,
    and the lofty city he brings down;
He tumbles it to the ground,
    levels it with the dust.
It is trampled underfoot by the needy,
    by the footsteps of the poor.

Isaiah 26:4-6

Or:

**B** Listen to the words of the prophet
Isaiah:

I am the LORD and there is no other,
there is no God besides me.

I form the light, and create the
darkness,
I make well-being and create woe;
I, the Lord, do all these things.
Let justice descend, O heavens, like dew
from above,
like gentle rain let the skies drop it
down.
Let the earth open and salvation bud
forth;
let justice also spring up!
I, the LORD, have created this.

Isaiah 45:5a,7-8

*The reader concludes:*

This is the Word of the Lord.

*All respond:*

Thanks be to God.

*The leader invites:*

Lift up your hearts.

*All respond:*

We lift them up to the Lord.

*Then the leader prays:*

God, the Father of mercies,
you willed your Son to take flesh,
in order to give life back to us.
Bless these your gifts
with which we are about to nourish our
    bodies,
so that, receiving new strength, we may
    wait in watchfulness
for the glorious coming of Christ.

We ask this through the same Christ our
    Lord.
R. Amen.

**AFTER THE MEAL**

*The leader says:*

Let us live soberly, justly, and devoutly in
    this world
as we wait in joyful hope
for the coming of our Savior, Jesus Christ.

*All respond:*

For the kingdom, the power, and the
glory are yours, now and for ever.

*See also the Advent Wreath blessing on page 110. On the last days before Christmas, the following prayers are added:*

December 17:
O Wisdom, O holy Word of God,
you govern all creation with
    your strong yet tender care.
Come and show your people the way to
    salvation.

December 18:
O sacred Lord of ancient Israel,
who showed yourself to Moses in the burning
    bush,
who gave him the holy law on Sinai mountain:
come, stretch out your mighty hand to set us
    free.

December 19:
O Flower of Jesse's stem,
you have been raised up as a sign for all peoples;
kings stand silent in your presence;
the nations bow down in worship before you.
Come, let nothing keep you from coming to our
    aid.

December 20:
O Key of David, O royal Power of Israel
    controlling at your will the gate of heaven:
come, break down the prison walls of death
    for those who dwell in darkness and the
        shadow of death;
and lead your captive people into freedom.

*December 21:*
O Radiant Dawn, splendor of eternal light,
  sun of justice:
come, shine on those who dwell in darkness
  and the shadow of death.

*December 22:*
O King of all the nations,
the only joy of every human heart;
O Keystone of the mighty arch of humankind,
come and save the creature you fashioned from
  the dust.

*December 23:*
O Emmanuel, king and lawgiver,
desire of the nations,
Savior of all people,
come and set us free, Lord our God.

# AT TABLE DURING CHRISTMASTIME

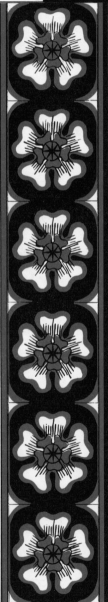

*A Christmas candle may be lighted as the leader says:*

Glory to God in the highest.

*All respond:*

And peace to his people on earth.

*The leader prays:*

Lord Jesus,
in the peace of this season
our spirits rejoice:
With the beasts and angels,
the shepherds and stars,
with Mary and Joseph
we sing God's praise.

By your coming
may the hungry be filled with
good things,
and may our table and home be
blessed.

Glory to God in the highest.

And peace to his people on earth.

*Another form of Christmas prayer begins with the sign of the cross.*

In the name of the Father, and of the Son, and of the Holy Spirit. Amen.

*Someone at table reads one of the following Scriptures or the text assigned to the liturgy of the day.*

**A** Listen to the words of the holy gospel according to John:

And the Word became flesh
and made his dwelling among us,
and we saw his glory,

the glory as of the Father's only Son,
full of grace and truth.

John 1:14

Or:

**B** Listen to the words of the prophet
Isaiah:

I rejoice heartily in the LORD,
in my God is the joy of my soul;
For he has clothed me with a robe of
salvation,
and wrapped me in a mantle of justice,
Like a bridegroom adorned with a
diadem,
like a bride bedecked with her jewels.
As the earth brings forth its plants,
and a garden makes its growth spring
up,
So will the LORD GOD make justice and
praise
spring up before all the nations.

Isaiah 61:10-11

*The reader concludes:*

This is the Word of the Lord.

*All respond:*

Thanks be to God.

*The leader invites:*

Lift up your hearts.

*All respond:*

We lift them up to the Lord.

*Then the leader prays:*

Blessed are you, Lord God.
Through the fruitful virginity of Mary
you fulfilled the long expectation
   of the poor and oppressed.
Grant that with the same faith
   with which Mary awaited the birth of
      her Son,
we may look for him in our brothers and
   sisters in need.

We ask this through Christ our Lord.
R. Amen.

**AFTER THE MEAL**

*The leader says:*

The Word became flesh, alleluia.

*All respond:*

And dwelt among us, alleluia.

# AT TABLE DURING THE WEEKDAYS OF LENT

*Begin after a short silence. The leader alternates with the others who are present.*

V. I was hungry.
R. And you gave me food.

V. I was thirsty.
R. And you gave me drink.

V. I was a stranger.
R. And you welcomed me.

V. I was naked.
R. And you clothed me.

V. I was ill.
R. And you comforted me.

V. I was in jail.
R. And you came to see me.

*The leader prays:*

Lord Jesus Christ,
may our lenten fasting turn us
    toward all our brothers and sisters who
    are in need.
Bless this table, our good food, and
    ourselves.
Send us through Lent with good cheer,
and bring us to the fullness of your
    passover.
R. Amen.

> *Another form of lenten prayer begins with the sign of the cross.*

In the name of the Father, and of the Son,
and of the Holy Spirit. Amen.

> *Someone at table reads one of the following Scriptures or the text assigned to the liturgy of the day.*

**A** Listen to the words of the apostle Paul to the Romans:

I urge you therefore, brothers [and sisters], by the mercies of God, to offer your bodies as a living sacrifice, holy and pleasing to God, your spiritual worship. Do not conform yourself to this age but be transformed by the renewal of your mind, that you may discern what is the will of God, what is good and pleasing and perfect.

Romans 12:1-2

Or:

**B** Listen to the words of the prophet Isaiah:

Wash yourselves clean!
Put away your misdeeds from before my eyes;
cease doing evil; learn to do good.
Make justice your aim: redress the wronged,
hear the orphan's plea, defend the widow.

Isaiah 1:16-17

Or:

C Listen to the words of the apostle Paul
to the Corinthians:

[God says:]

"In an acceptable time I heard you,
and on the day of salvation I helped
you."

Behold, now is a very acceptable time;
behold, now is the day of salvation. . . .
In everything we commend ourselves as
ministers of God, through much
endurance, in afflictions, hardships,
constraints, beatings, imprisonments,
riots, labors, vigils, fasts. . . . We are
treated as deceivers and yet are truthful;
as unrecognized and yet acknowledged; as
dying and behold we live; as chastised
and yet not put to death; as sorrowful yet
always rejoicing; as poor yet enriching
many; as having nothing and yet
possessing all things.

2 Corinthians 6:2,4-5,8-10

*The reader concludes:*

This is the Word of the Lord.

*All respond:*

Thanks be to God.

*The leader invites:*

Lift up your hearts.

*All respond:*

We lift them up to the Lord.

*Then the leader prays:*

We thank you, O Lord,
who give us this food to eat.
We pray that you may also provide food
for those who are hungry
and gather us all together
at the table of your heavenly kingdom.

We ask this through Christ our Lord.
R. Amen.

**AFTER THE MEAL**

*The leader says:*

No one lives on bread alone.

*All respond:*

But on every word that comes from the mouth of God.

# AT TABLE DURING THE EASTER TRIDUUM

From Holy Thursday evening until the great Vigil in the night between Holy Saturday and Easter, the catechumens and the baptized fast and pray and await the celebration of baptism. Any meals are very simple. "Let the paschal fast be kept sacred. Let it be observed everywhere on Good Friday and, where possible, prolonged throughout Holy Saturday, as a way of coming to the joys of the Sunday of the resurrection with uplifted and welcoming heart" (*Constitution on the Sacred Liturgy*, 110). The same prayer is used before and after meals.

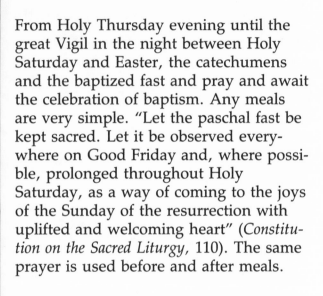

For our sake Christ was obedient,
    accepting even death, death on a
    cross.
Therefore God raised him on high
    and gave him the name above all
    other names.

# AT TABLE DURING EASTERTIME

*An Easter candle is lighted while the leader says:*

This is the day the Lord has made, alleluia!

*All respond:*

Let us rejoice and be glad, alleluia!

*The leader prays:*

We praise you, Lord, with greater joy than ever in this Easter season.
The thirsty have come to the water.
The poor have come to receive bread and eat.
Blessed are you in earth's bounty: the joy of the resurrection renews the whole world.

Christ is risen, alleluia!

*All respond:*

Christ is truly risen, alleluia!

*Another form of Easter prayer begins with the sign of the cross.*

In the name of the Father, and of the Son, and of the Holy Spirit. Amen.

*Someone at table reads one of the following Scriptures or the text assigned to the liturgy of the day.*

A   Listen to the words of the holy gospel according to John:

[When the disciples had returned to shore at the Sea of Tiberias,] they saw a charcoal fire with fish on it and bread. Jesus said to them, "Bring some of the fish you just caught." So Simon Peter went over and dragged the net ashore full of one hundred fifty-three large fish. Even though there were so many, the net was not torn. Jesus said to them, "Come, have breakfast." And none of the disciples dared to ask him, "Who are you?" because they realized it was the Lord. Jesus came over and took the bread and gave it to them, and in like manner the fish.

John 21:9-13

Or:

**B** Listen to the words of the holy gospel according to Luke:

[The two disciples urged Jesus,] "Stay with us, for it is nearly evening and the day is almost over." So he went in to stay with them. And it happened that, while he was with them at table, he took bread, said the blessing, broke it, and gave it to them. With that their eyes were opened and they recognized him.

Luke 24:29-31

Or:

C  Listen to the words of the apostle Peter:

Blessed be the God and Father of our
Lord Jesus Christ, who in his great mercy
gave us a new birth to a living hope
through the resurrection of Jesus Christ
from the dead.

1 Peter 1:3

*The reader concludes:*

This is the Word of the Lord.

*All respond:*

Thanks be to God.

*The leader invites:*

Lift up your hearts.

*All respond:*

We lift them up to the Lord.

*Then the leader prays:*

We joyfully sing your praises, Lord
   Jesus Christ.
Whom on the day of your resurrection
were recognized by your disciples
   in the breaking of the bread.

Remain here with us
as we gratefully partake of these gifts,
and at the banquet table in heaven
   welcome us,
who have welcomed you in our brothers
   and sisters,
for you live and reign for ever and ever.
Amen.

*All join in singing an alleluia.*

**AFTER THE MEAL**

*The leader says:*

The disciples recognized the Lord,
alleluia.

*All respond:*

In the breaking of the bread, alleluia.

*From Ascension to Pentecost, the leader says:*

Lord, send out your Spirit.

*All respond:*

And renew the face of the earth.

# AT BEDSIDE

*If several pray together, one leads the first prayers and all pray the Hail Mary together. Begin with the sign of the cross and say:*

May the all-powerful Lord grant us
  a restful night
and a peaceful death.

Protect us, Lord, as we stay awake;
watch over us as we sleep,
that awake, we may keep watch
  with Christ,
and asleep, rest in his peace.

Hail Mary, full of grace,
the Lord is with you!
Blessed are you among women,
and blessed is the fruit of your womb,
  Jesus.
Holy Mary, Mother of God,
pray for us sinners,
now and at the hour of our death.
R. Amen.

> *A longer form of night prayer begins with silence.
> This is an examination of conscience, a time to
> reflect on the day now past. Scripture texts which
> suggest the content of this examination of con-
> science include: Exodus 20:1-17; Matthew 5:1-11;
> Matthew 25:31-46; Ephesians 4:17-32; and
> Colossians 3:1-17. Then all pray the Confiteor:*

I confess to almighty God,
and to you, my brothers and sisters,
that I have sinned through my own fault
in my thoughts and in my words,
in what I have done,
and in what I have failed to do;

and I ask blessed Mary, ever virgin,
all the angels and saints,
and you, my brothers and sisters,
to pray for me to the Lord our God.

*Psalm 91, page 352, may be prayed. The
following hymn is also appropriate. It may be
sung to the tune called "Tallis Canon" or to "The
Old Hundreth" (Praise God from Whom All
Blessings Flow), or to another appropriate tune.*

All praise to thee, my God, this night,
For all the blessings of the light;
Keep me, O keep me, King of kings,
Beneath thine own almighty wings.

Forgive me, Lord, for thy dear Son,
The sin that I this day have done,
That with the world, myself and thee,
I, before sleep, at peace may be.

Teach me to live that I may dread
The grave as little as my bed;
Teach me to die that so I may
Rise glorious on that final day.

Thomas Ken

*The Canticle of Simeon may also be part of night
prayer:*

Lord, now you let your servant go in peace;
your word has been fulfilled:

my own eyes have seen the salvation
which you have prepared in the sight of every
   people:

a light to reveal you to the nations
and the glory of your people Israel.

Luke 2:29-32 (Nunc Dimittis)

*A period of silence may be observed, and prayers
of intercession and thanksgiving may be offered.*

*The leader then prays:*

Visit this house,
we beg you, Lord,
and banish from it
the deadly power of the evil one.
May your holy angels dwell here
to keep us in peace,
and may your blessing be always upon us.

We ask this through Christ our Lord.
R. Amen.

Or:

Lord Jesus Christ,
you have given your followers
an example of gentleness and humility,
a task that is easy, a burden that is light.
Accept the prayers and work of this day,
and give us the rest that will strengthen us
to render more faithful service to you
who live and reign for ever and ever.

*All invoke the protection of the Blessed Mother:*

A   Hail, holy Queen, mother of mercy,
hail, our life, our sweetness, and our hope.
To you we cry, the children of Eve;
to you we send up our sighs,
mourning and weeping in this land of exile.
Turn, then, most gracious advocate,
your eyes of mercy toward us;
lead us home at last
and show us the blessed fruit of your womb,
     Jesus:
O clement, O loving, O sweet Virgin Mary.

*Salve, Regina*

Or:

B   Mary, mother whom we bless,
full of grace and tenderness,
defend me from the devil's power
and greet me in my dying hour.

*The day ends, as it began, with the sign of the cross. A parent may sign a child's forehead or heart with the cross, saying one of these blessings:*

God bless you.

Praised be Jesus Christ!

The grace of the Lord Jesus be with [us] all.

Revelation 22:21

In the silent hours of night, bless the Lord.

Lord, bless this household and each one.
Place the cross of Christ on us with the power of
    your love
until we see the land of joy.

Christ is shepherd over you,
enfolding you on every side.
Christ will not forsake you hand or foot,
nor let evil come near you.


*Other night prayers of parent and child:*

Now I lay me down to sleep,
I pray the Lord my soul to keep.
Four corners to my bed,
Four angels there aspread:
Two to foot and two to head,
And four to carry me when I'm dead.
If any danger come to me,
Sweet Jesus Christ deliver me.
And if I die before I wake,
I pray the Lord my soul to take.

Angel sent by God to guide me,
be my light and walk beside me;
be my guardian and protect me;
on the paths of life direct me.

# PART II
# DAYS AND SEASONS

# INTRODUCTION
# THE CALENDAR

We know time not as flat and unchanging but as rhythms. Some of these are given by the planet that is our home: its rotation gives us days and nights; its inclination and its path around the sun give us seasons. Some rhythms come from ourselves, bodies and souls: we grow hungry and we eat; we grow tired and we rest; we pass through the measured stages of life. Yet other rhythms come from the communities in which we live, communities with stories to tell on certain days that we set aside.

Baptism brings us into a people who have given time a certain rhythm with words and deeds. These are the rites by which we mark each morning, each

Sunday, each Easter. Little by little, the observance of these times shapes us, leads us, puts into mind and heart and life the way of our people, the way of Jesus.

The Church has honored and kept the seven-day division of time received from the Jewish people and shared by many others. From the time of the apostles, the baptized have called the first day of the week the "Lord's Day." The week with its Sunday is the first and most important element of our calendar.

Influenced by the festivals and seasons of Judaism, and later by the calendars of other peoples and by their own needs (to initiate new members, for example), Christians came gradually to observe certain days and seasons. These have been kept with fasting or festivity, with songs and Scriptures and other readings, and with special practices that differ from one Christian community to another.

| | 1989 | 1990 | 1991 | 1992 | 1993 | 1994 | 1995 | 199 |
|---|---|---|---|---|---|---|---|---|
| ASH WEDNESDAY | Feb. 8 | Feb. 28 | Feb. 13 | March 4 | Feb. 24 | Feb. 16 | March 1 | Feb. |
| EASTER TRIDUUM | March 23-26 | April 12-15 | March 28-31 | April 16-19 | April 8-11 | March 31-April 3 | April 13-16 | April |
| ASCENSION | May 4 | May 24 | May 9 | May 28 | May 20 | May 12 | May 25 | May |
| PENTECOST | May 14 | June 3 | May 19 | June 7 | May 30 | May 22 | June 4 | May |
| ADVENT 1 | Dec. 3 | Dec. 2 | Dec. 1 | Nov. 29 | Nov. 28 | Nov. 27 | Dec. 3 | Dec. |

The yearly keeping of the passover of Christ—
the passion, death, and resurrection of the Lord—
became the time for the baptism of new Christians,
the very center of the Church's year. Around these
three days, called the "Easter Triduum," the seasons of Lent and the Fifty Days (Easter to Pentecost)
came to be observed with prayer and special practices.

Later, the solemnities of Christmas and Epiphany, with the preparatory season of Advent, were
kept with great festivity in the winter months. And
throughout the year, the Church in its local communities kept days in honor of Mary and the saints,
days in commemoration of events such as the ded-
ication of church buildings, and days in special
prayer or penance.

Listed below are the dates of the Paschal Season
and of the beginning of Advent over the next years.
The date of Easter is determined, like that of Passover, by the spring equinox and the full moon.

| 1997 | 1998 | 1999 | 2000 | 2001 | 2002 | 2003 | 2004 | 2005 |
|------|------|------|------|------|------|------|------|------|
| Feb. 12 | Feb. 25 | Feb. 17 | March 8 | Feb. 28 | Feb. 20 | Feb. 12 | March 3 | Feb. 16 |
| March 27-30 | April 9-12 | April 1-4 | April 20-23 | April 12-15 | April 4-7 | March 27-30 | April 15-18 | March 31-April 3 |
| May 8 | May 21 | May 13 | June 1 | May 24 | May 16 | May 8 | May 27 | May 12 |
| May 18 | May 31 | May 23 | June 11 | June 3 | May 26 | May 18 | June 6 | May 22 |
| Nov. 30 | Nov. 29 | Nov. 28 | Dec. 3 | Dec. 2 | Dec. 1 | Nov. 30 | Nov. 28 | Nov. 27 |

Advent's beginning is the fourth Sunday before December 25.

In some communities, the important dates of the year are announced in song on the solemnity of the Epiphany with the following words:

Dear brothers and sisters,
the glory of the Lord has shone upon us,
and shall ever be manifest among us,
until the day of his return.

Through the rhythms of times and seasons
let us celebrate the mysteries of salvation.

Let us recall the year's culmination,
the Easter Triduum of the Lord:
his crucifixion, his burial, and his rising
celebrated between the evening of
__(date of Holy Thursday)__
and the dawn of ___(date of Easter Sunday)___ .

Each Easter, each Sunday
the holy Church makes present that great
and saving deed
by which Christ has forever conquered sin
and death.

From Easter come forth and are reckoned
all the days we keep holy:
Ash Wednesday, the beginning of Lent, the
__(day)__ of __(month)__ ;
the Ascension of the Lord, the
__(day)__ of __(month)__ ;
Pentecost, the __(day)__ of __(month)__ ; and
the First Sunday of Advent, the
__(day)__ of __(month)__ .

Likewise, the pilgrim Church proclaims
the passover of Christ

in the feasts of the holy Mother of God,
in the feasts of the Apostles and Saints,
and in the commemoration of the faithful
   departed.

To Christ who was, who is, and who is to
   come,
Lord of time and history,
be endless praise, for ever and ever.

R. Amen.

Each year the Church keeps the feasts of the
saints and remembers the events of Jesus' life. A
calendar of these feasts and memorials is found
on page 401.

# ON SUNDAY

## INTRODUCTION

Remembering Jesus' death and resurrection and the coming of the Spirit, Christian Churches from apostolic times would gather on the first day of the week. It was the day of the new creation. It was the "eighth day," the day beyond the world's time. Christians have called it the "Lord's Day."

We have received this tradition. On the Lord's Day we come together, baptized and catechumens alike, to listen to our Scriptures. Then the baptized remain to intercede for all the world, to give God thanks and praise, and to share the Body and Blood of

Christ. We prepare for breaking this holy bread by fasting from other food, by remembering our baptism and pondering the Scriptures, and by setting aside a part of our own belongings for the poor and the Church.

*Table prayers for Sunday are on page 60. Other prayers for the Holy Eucharist are on page 359.*

Lord, by your cross and resurrection
you have set us free.
You are the Savior of the world.

Blessed be the God and Father of our Lord
    Jesus Christ,
who in his great mercy gave us a new birth to a
    living hope
through the resurrection of Jesus Christ from the
    dead.

1 Peter 1:3

Alleluia!
Jesus Christ is Lord!

## IN THE MORNING

It is good to give thanks to the LORD,
    to sing praise to your name, Most High,
To proclaim your kindness at dawn
    and your faithfulness throughout the night,
With ten-stringed instrument and lyre,
    with melody upon the harp.
For you make me glad, O LORD, by your deeds;

at the works of your hands I rejoice.

How great are your works, O LORD!
How very deep are your thoughts!

Psalm 92:2-6

## PREPARING TO JOIN THE ASSEMBLY FOR EUCHARIST

We shall go up with joy
to the house of our God.

Cf. Psalm 122:1

Then will I go in to the altar of God,
the God of my gladness and joy.

Psalm 43:4

## DURING THE COMMUNION FAST

How holy this feast
in which Christ is our food:
his passion is recalled,
grace fills our hearts,
and we receive a pledge of the glory to come.

Thomas Aquinas

## BEFORE STUDYING THE SUNDAY'S SCRIPTURE

A lamp to my feet is your word,
a light to my path.

Psalm 119:105

*The Sunday's Scriptures may be read by one alone or by the household. After the reading of the gospel, as the book is kissed, the following is prayed:*

May the words of the gospel wipe away our sins.

*After reading the Scriptures, the catechumens say:*

May the words of Scripture nourish us
and draw us to the waters of baptism.


## WHEN TAKING HOLY WATER

Blessed be God who has given us a new birth
by water and the Holy Spirit.


## WHEN SEEING OR REMEMBERING THE CATECHUMENS

Lord, look with love on the catechumens
through this time of preparation.
Enfold them within your Church.


## AT EVENING

Our God, we thank you for the joy and rest of
    this day.
May we yearn for the coming of your reign!

# ADVENT AND CHRISTMAS

## INTRODUCTION

Advent is a time of waiting, listening, holding back, and discovering the beauty in both the night and the day. Christmas is a festival that has many days: the Nativity itself; Saint Stephen; Saint John; Holy Innocents; Holy Family; Mary, Mother of God; Epiphany; and the Baptism of the Lord. The Christmas spirit springs from the delight and the terror of birth itself: the Word made flesh, the very presence of God with us. The "wonderful exchange," God sharing our human condition, and we caught up into God's grace, is the Church's reflection and song all through Advent and Christmas.

Year by year, we learn what it is to keep Advent: to take time with those days and nights before Christmas. And we learn too to keep Christmas: to make a festival of stories, songs, and deeds done year after year. Together the keeping of these seasons gives witness to how God reigns in our lives and in the world. Throughout these days of Advent and Christmas, the images of the nativity and of the final coming of our Messiah are placed side by side with the gospel we have believed: God-within us, now, in our brothers and sisters.

*Table prayers for Advent and Christmas are found on pages 64 and 70. The following blessings may be used at moments when the household has come together. The Sunday after Christmas is the feast of the Holy Family. On that day, the blessing of a family on page 206 is appropriate.*

# BLESSING OF AN ADVENT WREATH

The Advent wreath is made of four candles and a circle of branches. Before the first candle is lighted, the household gathers for this blessing.

*All make the sign of the cross. The leader begins:*

Our help is in the name of the Lord.

*All respond:*

Who made heaven and earth.

*The leader may use these or similar words to introduce the blessing:*

In the short days and long nights of Advent, we realize how we are always waiting for deliverance, always needing salvation by our God. Around this wreath, we shall remember God's promise.

*Then the Scripture is read:*

Listen to the words of the prophet Isaiah:

The people who walked in darkness
   have seen a great light;
Upon those who dwelt in the land of gloom
   a light has shone.
You have brought them abundant joy
   and great rejoicing.

Isaiah 9:1-2

*(The family's Bible may be used for an alternate reading, such as Isaiah 63:16-17 or Isaiah 64:2-7.)*

*The reader concludes:*

This is the Word of the Lord.

*All respond:*

Thanks be to God.

*After a time of silence, all join in prayers of intercession and in the Lord's Prayer.*

*Then the leader invites:*

Let us now pray for God's blessing upon us and upon this wreath.

*After a short silence, the leader prays:*

Lord our God,
we praise you for your Son, Jesus Christ:
he is Emmanuel, the hope of the peoples,
he is the wisdom that teaches and guides us,
he is the Savior of every nation.

Lord God,
let your blessing come upon us
as we light the candles of this wreath.
May the wreath and its light
be a sign of Christ's promise to bring us
   salvation.
May he come quickly and not delay.

We ask this through Christ our Lord.
R. Amen.

*The first candle is then lighted.*

*The leader says:*

Let us bless the Lord.

*All respond, making the sign of the cross:*

Thanks be to God.

*The blessing concludes with a verse from
"O Come, O Come, Emmanuel":*

O come, desire of nations, bind
In one the hearts of humankind;
Bid ev'ry sad divisions cease
And by thyself our Prince of peace.
Rejoice! Rejoice! Emmanuel
Shall come to thee, O Israel.

*Each day in Advent, perhaps at the evening meal
(see prayer on page 64), the candles are lighted:
one candle the first week, two the second, and so
forth.*

# BLESSING OF A CHRISTMAS TREE

When the tree has been prepared, the household gathers around it. All make the sign of the cross.

*The leader begins:*

Blessed be the name of the Lord.

*All respond:*

Now and for ever.

*The leader may use these or similar words to introduce the blessing:*

This tree is a blessing to our home. It reminds us of all that is beautiful, all that is filled with the gentleness and the promise of God. It stands in our midst as a tree of light that we might promise such beauty to one another and to our world. It stands like that tree of paradise that God made into the tree of life, the cross of Jesus.

*Then the Scripture is read:*

Listen to the words of the apostle Paul to Titus:

But when the kindness and generous love of
   God our savior appeared,
not because of any righteous deeds we had done
   but because of his mercy,

he saved us through the bath of rebirth
and renewal by the holy Spirit,
whom he richly poured out on us
through Jesus Christ our savior,
so that we might be justified by his grace
and become heirs in hope of eternal life.

Titus 3:4-7

*(The family's Bible may be used for an alternate reading such as Psalm 96:11-13.)*

*The reader concludes:*

This is the Word of the Lord.

*All respond:*

Thanks be to God.

*After a time of silence, all join in prayers of intercession and in the Lord's Prayer. Then the leader invites:*

Let us now pray for God's blessing upon all who gather around this tree.

*After a short silence, the leader prays:*

A   Lord our God,
we praise you for the light of creation:
the sun, the moon, and the stars of the night.
We praise you for the light of Israel:
the Law, the prophets, and the wisdom of
the Scriptures.

We praise you for Jesus Christ, your Son:
he is Emmanuel, God-with-us, the Prince of
    Peace,
who fills us with the wonder of your love.

Lord God,
let your blessing come upon us
as we illumine this tree.
May the light and cheer it gives
be a sign of the joy that fills our hearts.
May all who delight in this tree
come to the knowledge and joy of salvation.

We ask this through Christ our Lord.
R. Amen.

Or:

B   God of all creation,
    we praise you for this tree
    which brings beauty and memories and the
        promise of life to our home.
    May your blessing be upon all who gather
        around this tree,
    all who keep the Christmas festival by its
        lights.
    We wait for the coming of the Christ,
    the days of everlasting justice and of peace.
    You are our God, living and reigning, for ever
        and ever.
    R. Amen.

*The lights of the tree are then illuminated.*

*The leader says:*

Let us bless the Lord.

*All respond, making the sign of the cross:*

Thanks be to God.

*The blessing concludes with a verse from "O Come, O Come, Emmanuel":*

O come, thou dayspring, come and cheer
Our spirits by thine advent here;
Disperse the gloomy clouds of night
And death's dark shadow put to flight.
Rejoice! Rejoice! Emmanuel
Shall come to thee, O Israel.

# BLESSING OF A CHRISTMAS CRÈCHE
# OR MANGER SCENE

The manger scene has a special place near the Christmas tree or in another place where family members can reflect and pray during the Christmas season. It is blessed each year on Christmas Eve or Christmas Day.

*All make the sign of the cross. The leader begins:*

Our help is in the name of the Lord.

*All respond:*

Who made heaven and earth.

*The leader may use these or similar words to introduce the blessing:*

We are at the beginning of the days of Christmas. All through the season we will look on these images of sheep and cattle, of shepherds, of Mary and of Joseph and Jesus.

*Then the Scripture is read:*

Listen to the words of the holy gospel according to Luke:

In those days a decree went out from Caesar Augustus that the whole world should be enrolled. This was the first enrollment, when Quirinius was governor of Syria. So all went to be enrolled, each to his own town. And Joseph too went up from Galilee from the town of Nazareth to Judea, to the city of David that is called Bethlehem, because he was of the house and family of David, to be enrolled with Mary, his betrothed, who was with child. While they were there, the time came for her to have her child, and she gave birth to her firstborn son. She wrapped him in swaddling clothes and laid him in a manger, because there was no room for them in the inn.

Luke 2:1-7

*The reader concludes:*

This is the Gospel of the Lord.

*All respond:*

Praise to you, Lord Jesus Christ.

*The figures may be placed in the manger. After a time of silence, all join in prayers of intercession and in the Lord's Prayer.*

*Then the leader invites:*

Pray now for God's blessing as we look on these figures.

*After a short silence, the leader prays:*

A God of every nation and people,
from the very beginning of creation
you have made manifest your love:
when our need for a Savior was great
you sent your Son to be born of the
Virgin Mary.
To our lives he brings joy and peace,
justice, mercy, and love.

Lord,
bless all who look upon this manger;
may it remind us of the humble birth of Jesus,
and raise our thoughts to him,
who is God-with-us and Savior of all,
and who lives and reigns for ever and ever.
R. Amen.

Or:

B God of Mary and Joseph, of shepherds and
animals,
bless us whenever we gaze on this manger
scene.
Through all the days of Christmas
may these figures tell the story
of how humans, angels, and animals
found the Christ in this poor place.

Fill our house with hospitality, joy,
gentleness, and thanksgiving
and guide our steps in the way of peace.

Grant this through Christ our Lord.
R. Amen.

*The leader says:*

Let us bless the Lord.

*All respond, making the sign of the cross:*

Thanks be to God.

*Then Christmas songs and carols are sung,
for example:*

It came upon the midnight clear,
That glorious song of old,
From angels bending near the earth
To touch their harps of gold:
"Peace on the earth, good will to all
From heaven's all gracious King";
The world in solemn stillness lay,
To hear the angels sing.

Yet with the woes of sin and strife,
The world has suffered long;
Beneath the heav'nly hymn have rolled
Two thousand years of wrong;
And warring humankind hears not
The tidings which they bring;
O hush the noise and cease your strife
And hear the angels sing.

Edmond Sears (alt.)

# BLESSING FOR THE NEW YEAR

On New Year's Eve or New Year's Day, the household gathers at the table or at the Christmas tree or manger scene. Many people make New Year's Day a day of prayer for peace. The calendar of the new year may be held during the blessing.

*All make the sign of the cross. The leader begins:*

Let us praise the Lord of days and seasons and
  years, saying: Glory to God in the highest!

*All respond:*

And peace to his people on earth!

*The leader may use these or similar words to
introduce the blessing:*

Our lives are made of days and nights, of
seasons and years, for we are part of a universe
of suns and moons and planets. We mark ends
and we make beginnings and, in all, we praise
God for the grace and mercy that fill our days.

*Then the Scripture is read:*

Listen to the words of the book of Genesis:

God said: "Let there be lights in the dome of the sky, to separate day from night. Let them mark the fixed times, the days and the years, and serve as luminaries in the dome of the sky, to shed light upon the earth." And so it happened: God made the two great lights, the greater one to govern the day, and the lesser one to govern the night; and he made the stars. God set them in the dome of the sky, to shed light upon the earth, to govern the day and the night, and to separate the light from the darkness. God saw how good it was. Evening came, and morning followed—the fourth day.

Genesis 1:14-19

*(The family's Bible may be used for an alternate reading such as Psalm 90:1-4.)*

*The reader concludes:*

This is the Word of the Lord.

*All respond:*

Thanks be to God.

*After a time of silence, members of the household offer prayers of thanksgiving for the past year, and of intercession for the year to come. On January 1, it may be appropriate to conclude these prayers with the Litany of Loreto (page 343) since this is the solemn feast of Mary, Mother of God. In conclusion, all join hands for the Lord's Prayer.*

*Then the leader begins:*

Let us now pray for God's blessing in the new year.

*After a short silence, parents may place their hands on their children in blessing as the leader says:*

Remember us, O God;
from age to age be our comforter.
You have given us the wonder of time,
blessings in days and nights, seasons and years.

Bless your children at the turning of the year
and fill the months ahead with the bright hope
that is ours in the coming of Christ.

You are our God, living and reigning, for ever
     and ever.
R. Amen.

*Another prayer for peace may be said:*

Lord, make me an instrument of your peace:
where there is hatred, let me sow love;
where there is injury, pardon;
where there is doubt, faith;
where there is despair, hope;
where there is darkness, light;
where there is sadness, joy.

O divine Master, grant that I may not so much
    seek
to be consoled as to console,
to be understood as to understand,
to be loved as to love.
For it is in giving that we receive,
it is in pardoning that we are pardoned,
it is in dying that we are born to eternal life.
R. Amen.

St. Francis of Assisi

*The leader says:*

Let us bless the Lord.

*All respond, making the sign of the cross:*

Thanks be to God.

*Then the following verse may be sung to a tune such as "The Old Hundreth" (Praise God from Whom All Blessings Flow). It may be appropriate to exchange a greeting of peace or to join in toasts for the old and new year.*

Great God, we sing that mighty hand
By which supported still we stand;
The opening year your mercy showed;
That mercy crowns it till it close.

# BLESSING OF THE HOME AND HOUSEHOLD ON THE EPIPHANY

The traditional date of Epiphany is January 6, but in the United States it is celebrated on the Sunday between January 2 and January 8. Some communities have the custom of blessing homes while recalling the visit of the Magi. The household gathers at the manger scene.

*All make the sign of the cross. The leader begins:*

Peace be with this house and with all who live here. Blessed be the name of the Lord.

*All respond:*

Now and for ever.

*The leader may use these or similar words to introduce the blessing:*

During these days of the Christmas season, we keep this feast of Epiphany, celebrating the manifestation of Christ to the Magi, to John in the River Jordan, and to the disciples at the wedding at Cana. Today Christ is manifest to us! Today this home is a holy place.

*Then the Scripture is read:*

Listen to the words of the holy gospel according to John:

In the beginning was the Word,
   and the Word was with God,
   and the Word was God.
He was in the beginning with God.
All things came to be through him,
   and without him nothing came to be.

And the Word became flesh
   and made his dwelling among us,
   and we saw his glory,
   the glory as of the Father's only Son,
   full of grace and truth.

John 1:1-3,14

*(The family's Bible may be used for an alternate
reading such as Matthew 2:1-12.)*

*The reader concludes:*

This is the Gospel of the Lord.

*All respond:*

Praise to you, Lord Jesus Christ.

*Everyone then processes from one room to
another. In each room, God's blessing is asked on
all that takes place in that room. Blessed water
may be carried and sprinkled. When all return to
the starting place, they join in the Lord's Prayer.*

*Then the leader begins:*

Let us pray.

*After a short silence, the leader continues:*

A   Lord God of heaven and earth,
    you revealed your only-begotten Son to every
        nation
    by the guidance of a star.

    Bless this house
    and all who inhabit it.

    Fill them (us) with the light of Christ,
    that their (our) concern for others may reflect
        your love.

    We ask this through Christ our Lord.
    R. Amen.

Or:

B   Lord our God, bless this household.
    May we be blessed with health, goodness of
        heart,
    gentleness, and the keeping of your law.
    We give thanks to you,
    Father, Son, and Holy Spirit,
    now and for ever.
    R. Amen.

*The leader says:*

**Let us bless the Lord.**

*All respond, making the sign of the cross:*

**Thanks be to God.**

*The blessing concludes with an appropriate song, for example, "O Come, All Ye Faithful" or "We Three Kings."*

# PASCHAL TIME
# LENT, EASTER, PENTECOST

## INTRODUCTION

At the center of our year's cycle is the Easter Triduum. These three days begin on the night of Holy
Thursday, culminate in the great Vigil kept in the
darkness between Saturday and Sunday, and end
with evening prayer on Easter Sunday.

On Good Friday and Holy Saturday the Church,
remembering the paschal mystery of Jesus' death
and resurrection, fasts and prays and prepares for
the Vigil. On that night the gathered community
spends much time in attending to the Scriptures;

then in the sacraments of initiation—baptism, confirmation, eucharist—we celebrate Christ's resurrection in our very midst.

For fifty days, from Easter to Pentecost, the Church keeps "the Great Sunday of the Year." Baptism and confirmation and eucharist, celebrated at the Vigil, now give light and guidance to the whole of life.

From Ash Wednesday to Holy Thursday, the Church keeps a time of penance and preparation for baptism. The catechumens are now the "elect," chosen for initiation at the great Vigil of Easter, and those who are already baptized strive to recover and renew what has happened to them: in baptism, we have put on Christ.

*Table prayers for the paschal season are found on page 76, page 82, and page 84. The blessings that follow are for the household during these days. During Lent, the prayers for times of penance and reconciliation on page 315 are appropriate. Prayers for the sacrament of penance are on page 248.*

# ASH WEDNESDAY
# BLESSING OF THE SEASON
# AND OF A PLACE OF PRAYER

From Ash Wednesday to Pentecost, a place in the home is set aside for prayer. The family's Bible is placed there with a cross and a candle, which is lighted when all have gathered.

*All make the sign of the cross as the leader begins:*

The Lord calls us to days of penance and mercy.
Blessed be the name of the Lord.

*All respond:*

Now and for ever.

*The leader may use these or similar words to introduce the blessing:*

Remember that we are but dust and ashes, yet by God's grace we have died in baptism and have put on the Lord Jesus Christ. Each year we keep these Forty Days with prayer and penance and the practice of charity so that we may come to the Easter festival ready to renew once more the life-giving commitment of our baptism. Through this Lent we shall gather here to read the Scriptures and ponder them and to intercede with God for the needs of the world.

*Then the Scripture is read:*

Listen to the words of the prophet Isaiah:

Is this the manner of fasting I wish,
   of keeping a day of penance:
That a man bow his head like a reed,
   and lie in sackcloth and ashes?
Do you call this a fast,
   a day acceptable to the LORD?
This, rather, is the fasting that I wish:
   releasing those bound unjustly,
   untying the thongs of the yoke;
Setting free the oppressed,
   breaking every yoke;
Sharing your bread with the hungry,
   sheltering the oppressed and the homeless;
Clothing the naked when you see them,
   and not turning your back on your own.

Then your light shall break forth like the dawn,
   and your wound shall quickly be healed;
Your vindication shall go before you,
   and the glory of the LORD shall be your rear
   guard.
Then you shall call, and the LORD will answer,
   you shall cry for help, and he will say: Here
   I am!
If you remove from your midst oppression,
   false accusation and malicious speech;
If you bestow your bread on the hungry
   and satisfy the afflicted;
Then light shall rise for you in the darkness,
   and the gloom shall become for you like
   midday.

Isaiah 58:5-10

*(The family's Bible may be used for an alternate reading such as Deuteronomy 30:15-20.)*

*The reader concludes:*

This is the Word of the Lord.

*All respond:*

Thanks be to God.

*After a time of silence, members of the household offer prayers of intercession for the world, the Church and its catechumens, and themselves. The leader then invites:*

Let us kneel and ask God's blessing on us and on this holy season.

*After a short silence, the leader continues:*

Merciful God,
you called us forth from the dust of the earth;
you claimed us for Christ in the waters of
    baptism.
Look upon us as we enter these Forty Days
bearing the mark of ashes,
and bless our journey through the desert of Lent
to the font of rebirth.
May our fasting be hunger for justice;
our alms, a making of peace;
our prayer, the chant of humble and grateful
    hearts.

All that we do and pray is in the name of Jesus,
for in his cross you proclaim your love
for ever and ever.
R. Amen.

*Each person then kisses the cross.*

*All then stand, and the leader concludes:*

All through these days let us be quiet and
prayerful, pondering the mysteries told in the
Scriptures. In the cross, we have been claimed for
Christ. In Christ, we make the prayer that fills
these days of mercy:

Our Father . . .
For the kingdom, the power, and the glory
   are yours, now and for ever. Amen.

*The leader says:*

Let us bless the Lord.

*All respond, making the sign of the cross:*

Thanks be to God.

*The blessing may conclude with an appropriate
song. The following may be sung to a tune such
as "The Old Hundreth" (Praise God from Whom
All Blessings Flow) or "Erhalt Uns Herr" (The
Glory of These Forty Days).*

Again we keep this solemn fast,
A gift of faith from ages past,
This Lent which binds us lovingly
To faith and hope and charity.

More sparing, therefore, let us make
The words we speak, the food we take,
Our sleep, our laughter, ev'ry sense;
Learn peace through holy penitence.

Gregory the Great

# BLESSINGS OF LENTEN DISCIPLINES FASTING, ALMSGIVING

For these Forty Days we are conscious of how we must sharpen our senses and focus mind and heart on the reign of God. We are, above all, aware of those waters in which we were baptized into Christ's death. That is, death to sin and evil; it is life in Christ that we began in those waters of baptism. These waters wait at Lent's end for the catechumens. The Church asks us to give ourselves to prayer and to the reading of Scripture, to fasting and to giving alms. The fasting that all do together on Fridays is but a sign of the daily lenten discipline of individuals and households: fasting for certain periods of time, fasting from certain foods, but also fasting from other things and activities. Likewise, the giving of alms is some effort to share this world equally not only through the distribution of money, but through the sharing of our time and possessions and through work of many kinds for a just world.

*The words of blessing on page 315 may also be used at these times.*

Blessed are you, Lord, God of all creation:
you make us hunger and thirst for holiness.
Blessed are you, Lord, God of all creation:
you call us to true fasting:
to set free the oppressed,
to share our bread with the hungry,
to shelter the homeless and to clothe the naked.

Withered and dried up like grass is my heart;
I forget to eat my bread.
Because of my insistent sighing
I am reduced to skin and bone.
I am like a desert owl;
I have become like an owl among the ruins.
I am sleepless, and I moan;
I am like a sparrow alone on the housetop.

For I eat ashes like bread
and mingle my drink with tears.

But you, O LORD, abide forever,
and your name through all generations.

Psalm 102:5-8,10,13

## BEFORE A TIME OF SOLITUDE

Blessed are you, Lord, God of all creation:
you manifest yourself when we are silent.

## BEFORE DEEDS OF CHARITY

Blessed are you, Lord, God of all creation:
for all the earth is yours.

*During Lent, the following hymn may be sung to any appropriate tune.*

The glory of these Forty Days
We celebrate with songs of praise;
For Christ, through whom all things were made,
Himself has fasted and has prayed.

Alone and fasting Moses saw
The loving God who gave the Law;
And to Elijah, fasting, came
The steeds and chariots of flame.

So Daniel trained his mystic sight,
Delivered from the lions' might;
And John, the Bridegroom's friend, became
The herald of Messiah's name.

Then grant us, Lord, like them to be
Full oft in fast and prayer with thee;
Our spirits strengthen with thy grace,
And give us joy to see thy face.

Gregory the Great

# PASSION SUNDAY: PLACING OF BRANCHES IN THE HOME

The branches that are blessed and brought home on Passion (Palm) Sunday are placed near the cross and Scriptures. They remind us that Lent is the slow coming of spring to the earth, the renewal of life. They are like the great "Hosanna" with which we hail the crucified and risen Lord.

After dinner or at another time on Palm Sunday, the household gathers where the palms have been placed with the cross and Scriptures.

*All make the sign of the cross. The leader begins:*

Hosanna in the highest!
Blessed is he who comes in the name of the
Lord.

*All respond:*

Hosanna in the highest!

*The leader may use these or similar words to introduce the prayer:*

We have come to the last days of Lent. Today we heard the reading of the Passion. That story will remain with us as we leave Lent behind on Holy Thursday and enter into the Three Days when we celebrate the mystery of Christ passing through suffering and death to life at God's right hand.

*Then the Scripture is read:*

Listen to the words of the apostle Paul to the Corinthians:

[We are] always carrying about in the body the dying of Jesus, so that the life of Jesus may also be manifested in our body. For we who live are constantly being given up to death for the sake of Jesus, so that the life of Jesus may be manifested in our mortal flesh.

2 Corinthians 4:10-11

*The reader concludes:*

This is the Word of the Lord.

*All respond:*

Thanks be to God.

> *After a time of silence, members of the household join in prayers of intercession, or the Litany of the Holy Name of Jesus, page 335, may be prayed. After the Lord's Prayer, the leader begins:*

Let us pray.

Blessed are you, God of Israel,
so rich in love and mercy.
Let these branches ever remind us of Christ's
   triumph.
May we who bear them rejoice in his cross
and sing your praise for ever and ever.
R. Amen.

*Together all take the palms to the place where they will be kept through the coming year. The following hymn may be sung to a tune such as "The Old Hundreth" (Praise God from Whom All Blessings Flow) or "Erhalt Uns Herr" (The Glory of These Forty Days).*

O Sun of justice, Jesus Christ,
Dispel the darkness of our hearts,
Till your blest light makes nighttime flee
And brings the joys your day imparts.

The day, your day, in beauty dawns
When in your light earth blooms anew;
Led back again to life's true way,
May we, forgiv'n, rejoice in you.

*The leader says:*

Let us bless the Lord.

*All respond, making the sign of the cross:*

Thanks be to God.

# PRAYERS OF THE TRIDUUM

"Christ redeemed us all and gave perfect glory to God principally through his paschal mystery: dying he destroyed our death and rising he restored our life. Therefore the Easter Triduum of the passion and resurrection of Christ is the culmination of the entire liturgical year. . . . The Easter Triduum begins with the evening Mass of the Lord's Supper (on Holy Thursday), reaches its high point in the Easter Vigil, and closes with evening prayer on Easter Sunday. On Good Friday and, if possible, also on Holy Saturday until the Easter Vigil, the Easter fast is observed everywhere." (*General Norms for the Liturgical Year*, nos. 18-19)

Thus does the Church's calendar speak of these Three Days. Lent ends on Holy Thursday. Friday and Saturday are days of private and communal prayer, of strict fasting from food and work and entertainment. This is in anticipation of the great Vigil when the catechumens at last are baptized, confirmed, and join in the eucharistic banquet. This fasting from food and work and entertainment is not sad and penitential. It is rather a fasting of eager excitement as we approach the Vigil with its Scripture, the baptism, the renewal of our passover. Thus are the death and resurrection of Christ proclaimed in our midst. At various moments from Thursday evening until Sunday, the community gathers for prayer and vigil: each parish community together keeps these holy days.

## HOLY THURSDAY EVENING

Lent ends quietly on this evening as we move into the great Three Days that are called "Passover" or "Easter." The liturgy of this night proclaims that we find glory in the cross: This mystery gathers us to watch and pray from now until Easter Sunday. The first song of this night's liturgy will echo through every moment of the Three Days:

We should glory in the cross of our Lord
   Jesus Christ,
for he is our salvation, our life, and our
   resurrection;
through him we are saved and made free.

See Galatians 6:14

*We enter the Three Days in a peculiar way: washing feet, letting our feet be washed. This is an ancient meditation on what we do:*

Jesus, come, my feet are dirty. You have become a servant for my sake, so fill your basin with water; come, wash my feet. I know that I am bold in saying this, but your own words have made me fearful: "If I do not wash your feet, you will have no companionship with me."

Wash my feet, then, so that I may be your companion.

But what am I saying: "Wash my feet"? Peter could say these words, for all that needed washing were his feet. For the rest, he was completely clean. I must be made clean with that other washing of which you said: "I have a baptism with which I must be baptized."

Origen

*After the evening liturgy, it is customary to spend time in prayer. Prayers before the blessed sacrament are in Part V (page 359). Thus begins the watching and praying of these Three Days. Among the Scriptures that are appropriate for reading and reflection are John, chapters 14 to 17, Psalm 22, and the Book of Lamentations.*

## GOOD FRIDAY

Today and tomorrow the Church takes on the Paschal Fast, the Easter Fast. This is not a fast of penance but of anticipation. It is fasting like the fasting of a bride or groom before the wedding, a fasting of excitement when we are so filled with anticipation that we cannot eat. We fast also from work and from all the usual distractions. Minds and hearts grow hungry for God's word. Our lives are filled instead with the mystery of Jesus' death and resurrection, with how we ourselves take on that dying and rising, little by little becoming the image of Christ in this world. On Friday afternoon or evening, the parish community gathers to read the Passion, to pray, and to venerate the Holy Cross. These are prayers and songs of Good Friday.

Lord, send your abundant blessing upon your
    people
who devoutly recall the death of your Son
in the sure hope of the resurrection.
Grant us pardon; bring us comfort.
May our faith grow stronger
and our eternal salvation be assured.


We worship you, Lord,
we venerate your cross,
we praise your resurrection.
Through the cross you brought joy to the world.


Holy is God!
Holy and strong!
Holy immortal One,
have mercy on us!


This is the wood of the cross,
on which hung the Savior of the world.
Come, let us worship.


How splendid the cross of Christ!
It brings life, not death;
light, not darkness;
Paradise, not its loss.
It is the wood on which the Lord,
like a great warrior,
was wounded in hands and feet and side,
but healed thereby our wounds.
A tree had destroyed us,
a tree now brought us life.

Theodore of Studios

## HOLY SATURDAY

The Paschal Fast begun on Thursday night continues today. The Church puts aside work and food
to continue watching and praying. The prayers
above for Good Friday are fitting. Other prayers for
Holy Saturday are given here. The first text is from
a centuries-old homily for Holy Saturday. The final
prayer below is for those who are to be baptized
this night.

He has gone to search for our first parent, as
for a lost sheep. Greatly desiring to visit those
who live in darkness and in the shadow of
death, he has gone to free from sorrow the
captives Adam and Eve, he who is both God
and the son of Eve. The Lord approached them
bearing the cross, the weapon that had won
him the victory. At the sight of him Adam, the
first man he had created, struck his breast in
terror and cried out to everyone: "My Lord be
with you all." Christ answered him: "And with
your spirit." He took him by the hand and
raised him up, saying, "Awake, O sleeper, and
rise from the dead, and Christ will give you
light."

Rise, let us leave this place. The enemy led you
out of the earthly paradise. I will not restore
you to that paradise, but I will enthrone you in
heaven. I forbade you the tree that was only a
symbol of life, but see, I who am life itself am
now one with you. I appointed cherubim to
guard you as slaves are guarded, but now I
make them worship you as God. The throne
formed by cherubim awaits you, its bearers

swift and eager. The bridal chamber is
adorned, the banquet is ready, the eternal
dwelling places are prepared, the treasure
houses of all good things lie open. The
kingdom of heaven has been prepared for you
from all eternity.


O Christ,
you slept a life-giving sleep in the grave,
and didst awakened humankind from the heavy
sleep of sin.


All-powerful and ever-living God,
your only Son went down among the dead
and rose again in glory.
In your goodness raise up your faithful people
buried with him in baptism,
to be one with him
in the eternal life of heaven.


Lord,
we pray to you for the elect,
who have now accepted for themselves
the loving purpose and the mysteries
that you revealed in the life of your Son.
May they have faith in their hearts
and accomplish your will in their lives.

We ask this through Christ our Lord.
R. Amen.

# THE EASTER VIGIL

The Church gathers tonight hungry for God's word. We keep vigil, listening to the Scriptures unfold their stories of creation and liberation, their prophecies of God's bounty and love, their demand that we acknowledge our baptism into the death of Christ. We sing again the alleluia, and the gospel of Christ's resurrection is heard. Only then does the Church call on all the saints and process to the font. There our catechumens, the elect, reject evil and profess their faith in Father, Son, and Spirit. They are baptized and then anointed with chrism. The whole Church rejoices. New Christians and old then join in the eucharist. The texts below reflect various moments in the liturgy of this night. Forms of the creed and the renunciations and baptismal promises will be found on page 371.

Night devoid of all dark,
O night dispelling sleep
and teaching us the vigilance of angels,
O night the demons tremble at,
night of all nights in all the year desired.

Asterius of Amasia

Rejoice, heavenly powers! Sing, choirs of angels!
Exult, all creation around God's throne!
Jesus Christ, our King, is risen!
Sound the trumpet of salvation!

Rejoice, O earth, in shining splendor,
radiant in the brightness of your King!
Christ has conquered! Glory fill you!
Darkness vanishes for ever!

O happy fault, O necessary sin of Adam,
which gained for us so great a Redeemer!

The power of this holy night
dispels all evil, washes guilt away,
restores lost innocence, brings mourners joy;
it casts out hatred, brings us peace,
and humbles earthy pride.

Night truly blessed when heaven is wedded to
    earth
and we are reconciled with God!

*Exsultet*

Alleluia!

What did you say then, each of you, as you stood there? "I renounce you, Satan, wicked and cruel tyrant!" And you asserted: "Henceforth, I am no longer in your power. For Christ destroyed that power by sharing with me a nature of flesh and blood. He destroyed death by dying; never again shall I be enslaved by you. I renounce you, crafty serpent full of deceit! I renounce you who lurk in ambush, who pretend friendship but have been the cause of every iniquity, who instigated the sin of our first parents! I renounce you, Satan, author and abettor of every evil." Do you understand, then, how Christ has united his bride to himself and what food he gives us all to eat? By one and the same food we are both brought into being and nourished. As a woman nourishes her child with her own blood and milk, so does Christ unceasingly nourish with his own blood those to whom he himself has given life.

Cyril of Jerusalem

## EASTER SUNDAY

The Three Days continue until the evening of Sunday. And at the same time, the Church begins the Fifty Days, the time of rejoicing between Easter and Pentecost. Here are songs and greetings for Easter Sunday and the Easter season.

V. This is the day the Lord has made;
R. let us rejoice and be glad. Alleluia.

V. Christ is risen, alleluia!
R. Christ is truly risen, alleluia!

# BLESSING OF EASTER FOODS

After the fasting of Lent, and the Easter Fast from Thursday night until the Vigil, the foods of Easter have a special place. The following blessing prayer may be used with the table prayer for Easter (page 84) before the meal that breaks the Easter Fast.

God of glory,
the eyes of all turn to you
as we celebrate Christ's victory over sin and death.

Bless + us and this food of our first Easter meal.
May we who gather at the Lord's table,
continue to celebrate the joy of his resurrection
and be admitted finally to his heavenly banquet.

Grant this through Christ our Lord.
R. Amen.

# BLESSING OF HOMES DURING EASTERTIME

In some communities, it is customary for homes to be blessed during the Easter season. All who live in the house should be present along with friends and neighbors. The leader may be a minister from the parish or a member of the household.

*All make the sign of the cross. The leader begins:*

God fills our hearts and homes with peace.
Blessed be the name of the Lord.

*All respond:*

Now and for ever.

*The leader may use these or similar words to introduce the blessing:*

Christ, risen from the dead, is our hope, joy, and comfort. May all who enter this home find Christ's light and love.

Listen to the words of the holy gospel according to Luke:

As [the two disciples and Jesus] approached the village [of Emmaus, Jesus] gave the impression that he was going on farther. But they urged him, "Stay with us, for it is nearly evening and the day is almost over." So he went in to stay with them. And it happened that, while he was with them at table, he took bread, said the blessing, broke it, and gave it to them. With that their eyes were opened and they recognized him, but he vanished from their sight. Then they said to each other, "Were not our hearts burning [within us] while he spoke to us on the way and opened the scriptures to us?"

Luke 24:28-32

*(The family's Bible may be used for an alternate reading such as John 20:19-21.)*

*The reader concludes:*

This is the Gospel of the Lord.

*All respond:*

Praise to you, Lord Jesus Christ.

*Intercessions may be made while going from room to room or around the outside of the house. This prayer may be said at the front door:*

O God,
make the door of this house wide enough
to receive all who need human love and
    fellowship,
narrow enough to shut out all envy, pride, and
    strife.
Make its threshold smooth enough
to be no stumbling-block to children, nor to
    straying feet,
but rugged and strong enough to turn back the
    tempter's power.
God, make the door of this house the gateway
    to your eternal kingdom.

Grant this through Christ our Lord.
R. Amen.

> *The house and rooms and family may be sprinkled
> with holy water, a reminder of baptism during the
> Easter season. The procession and intercessions
> conclude with the Lord's Prayer. The leader then
> speaks the prayer of blessing:*

Lord,
we rejoice in the victory of your Son over death:
by rising from the tomb to new life
he gives us new hope and promise.
Bless all the members of this household
and surround them with your protection,
that they may find comfort and peace
in Jesus Christ, the paschal lamb,
who lives and reigns with you and the
    Holy Spirit,
one God, for ever and ever.
R. Amen.

*All make the sign of the cross as the leader concludes:*

May Christ Jesus dwell with us,
keep us from all harm,
and make us one in mind and heart,
now and for ever.
R. Amen.

*The blessing may conclude with song. The following may be sung to any appropriate tune.*

Christ the Lord is ris'n today, Alleluia!
All on earth and angels say, Alleluia!
Raise your joys and triumphs high, Alleluia!
Sing, O heavens, and earth reply, Alleluia!

Love's redeeming work is done, Alleluia!
Fought the fight, the battle won. Alleluia!
Death in vain forbids him rise, Alleluia!
Christ has opened paradise. Alleluia!

Charles Wesley

# PENTECOST PRAYERS

Pentecost, the fiftieth day, concludes the season of Easter. The first prayer may be used on all the days between Ascension and Pentecost. On Pentecost itself, "Holy Spirit, Lord Divine" is sung and prayed over all that the Spirit does in our midst.

V. Come, Holy Spirit, fill the hearts of your faithful.
R. And kindle in them the fire of your love.

V. Send forth your Spirit and they shall be created.
R. And you will renew the face of the earth.

Let us pray.

Lord,
by the light of the Holy Spirit
you have taught the hearts of your faithful.
In the same Spirit
help us to relish what is right
and always rejoice in your consolation.

We ask this through Christ our Lord.
R. Amen.

Holy Spirit, Lord Divine,
Come, from heights of heav'n and shine,
  Come with blessed radiance bright!
Come, O Father of the poor,
Come, whose treasured gifts endure,
  Come, our heart's unfailing light!

Of consolers, wisest, best,
And our souls' most welcome guest,
  Sweet refreshment, sweet repose.
In our labor rest most sweet,
Pleasant coolness in the heat,
  Consolation in our woes.

Light most blessed, shine with grace
In our heart's most secret place,
  Fill your faithful through and through!
Left without your presence here,
Life itself would disappear,
  Nothing thrives apart from you!

Cleanse our soiled hearts of sin,
Arid souls refresh within,
  Wounded lives to health restore!
Bend the stubborn heart and will,
Melt the frozen, warm the chill,
  Guide the wayward home once more!

On the faithful who are true
And profess their faith in you,
  In your sev'n-fold gift descend!
Give us virtue's sure reward,
Give us your salvation, Lord,
  Give us joys that never end! Amen.

*Veni Sancte Spiritus*

# FEASTS AND FASTS

## INTRODUCTION

Throughout the year, especially during those weeks that are not part of the Advent/Christmas season or the Paschal season, the Church keeps certain days in memory of the saints (see page 401), other days of special intercession or blessing, other days of fasting and repentance. Several of these feast days and fast days are given here with appropriate prayers or blessings.

# THIRD WEEK IN JANUARY: WEEK OF PRAYER FOR CHRISTIAN UNITY

Gracious Father,
we pray to you for your holy catholic Church.
Fill it with your truth.
Keep it in your peace.
Where it is corrupt, reform it.
Where it is in error, correct it.
Where it is right, defend it.
Where it is in want, provide for it.
Where it is divided, reunite it;
for the sake of your Son, our Savior Jesus Christ.
R. Amen.

William Laud

*Another prayer for unity:*

Almighty and eternal God,
you gather the scattered sheep
and watch over those you have gathered.

Look kindly on all who follow Jesus, your Son.
You have marked them with the seal of one
    baptism,
now make them one in the fullness of faith
and unite them in the bond of love.

We ask this through Christ our Lord.
R. Amen.

# CANDLEMAS: RECEIVING BLESSED CANDLES AT HOME

On February 2, forty days after Christmas, the Church celebrates the feast of the Presentation of the Lord (see Luke 2:22-40). Because it echoes the Christmas festival, this day is a celebration of light in darkness. Its gospel tells of the old man Simeon calling the infant Jesus a "light to the Gentiles and the glory of your people Israel." For nine centuries, it has been traditional to bless candles on this day. Because of its simplicity and beauty, the candle has continued to be used when the Church gathers for prayer, both in public places and in the home. Candles blessed at the liturgy may be brought into the home with the rite that follows. One or more of the candles is lighted; others are placed nearby. These candles are lighted at ordinary times (at dinner, for example) and at special times such as during the anointing of the sick or when communion is brought to a member of the family.

*All make the sign of the cross. The leader begins:*

Jesus Christ is the light of the world,
a light no darkness can overpower.
Blessed be the name of the Lord.

*All respond:*

Now and for ever.

*The leader may use these or similar words to introduce the blessing:*

These candles bring beauty and light to our home. In the darkness, they tell us of God's gift of light and of Christ, whose light we received at baptism.

*Then the Scripture is read:*

Listen to the words of the holy gospel according to Luke:

There was a man in Jerusalem whose name was Simeon. This man was righteous and devout, awaiting the consolation of Israel, and the holy Spirit was upon him. . . . He came in the Spirit into the temple; and when the parents brought in the child Jesus to perform the custom of the law in regard to him, he took him into his arms and blessed God, saying:

> "Now, Master, you may let your servant go
>     in peace, according to your word,
> for my eyes have seen your salvation,
>     which you prepared in sight of all the
>     peoples,
> a light for revelation to the Gentiles,
>     and glory for your people Israel."

Luke 2:25,27-32

*The reader concludes:*

This is the Gospel of the Lord.

*All respond:*

Praise to you, Lord Jesus Christ.

*After a time of silence, all hold lighted candles as the leader begins:*

Let us pray.

God of night and of day,
we praise you for the brightness of our sun,
for the softer light of the moon
and the splendor of the stars,
for the fires of earth that bring us light and
    warmth
even as they imperil all who use them.
By the great and small lights we mark our days
    and seasons,
we brighten the night and bring warmth to our
    winter,
and in these lights we see light:
Jesus, whose light we receive in baptism,
whose light we carry by day and by night.

In the beauty of these candles,
keep us in quiet and in peace,
keep us safe and turn our hearts to you
that we may ourselves be light for our world.

All praise be yours through Christ,
the light of nations,
the glory of Israel,
for ever and ever.
R. Amen.

*The leader says:*

Let us bless the Lord.

*All respond, making the sign of the cross:*

Thanks be to God.

*The service may conclude with song. The following may be sung to the "Hymn to Joy" (Joyful, Joyful, We Adore Thee).*

Thy strong word did cleave the darkness;
At the speaking it was done;
For created light we thank thee,
While thine ordered seasons run:
Alleluia! Alleluia!
Praise to thee, who light dost send!
Alleluia! Alleluia!
Alleluia without end!

Martin Franzmann

# SAINT JOSEPH

In some communities, a feast is prepared on March 19, the solemnity of Saint Joseph, to be shared with all, especially the poor. The Litany of Saint Joseph is on page 346.

Father,
you entrusted our Savior to the care of
   Saint Joseph.
By the help of his prayers
may your Church continue to serve its Lord,
   Jesus Christ,
who lives with you and the Holy Spirit,
one God, for ever and ever.
R. Amen.

# ROGATION DAYS: BLESSING OF FIELDS AND GARDENS

The Rogation Days were traditionally celebrated on the three days before the solemnity of the Ascension. They may now be celebrated at any time when it is appropriate to ask that gardens, fields, and orchards be blessed during the coming season. The blessing takes place in the midst of the garden or field.

*All make the sign of the cross. The leader begins:*

Let us together praise the Lord,
from whom we have rain from the heavens
and abundance from the earth.
Blessed be God now and for ever.

*All respond:*

Amen.

*The leader may use these or similar words to introduce the blessing:*

Let us bless God, whose might has created the earth and whose providence has enriched it. God has given us the earth to cultivate, so that we may gather its fruits to sustain life. As we thank God for this bounty, let us learn also, as the Gospel teaches, to seek first God's way of holiness: then all we need will be given us besides.

*Then the Scripture is read:*

Listen to the words of the book of Genesis:

In the beginning, when God created the heavens and the earth, . . .

God said, "Let the earth bring forth vegetation: every kind of plant that bears seed and every kind of fruit tree on earth that bears fruit with its seed in it." And so it happened: the earth brought forth every kind of plant that bears seed and every kind of fruit tree on earth that bears fruit with its seed in it. God saw how good it was.

God also said: "See, I give you every seed-bearing plant all over the earth and every tree that has seed-bearing fruit on it to be your food; and to all the animals of the land, all the birds of the air, and all the living creatures that crawl on the ground, I give all the green plants for food." And so it happened. God looked at everything he had made, and he found it very good. Evening came, and morning followed—the sixth day.

Genesis 1:1,11-12,29-31

*(The family's Bible may be used for an alternate reading such as Mark 4:26-29.)*

*The reader concludes:*

This is the Word of the Lord.

*All respond:*

Thanks be to God.

*After a time of silence, the prayers of intercession may take the form of the Litany of the Saints (page 348). This may be chanted while processing through the garden or fields.*

*Then the leader prays:*

O God,
from the very beginning of time
you commanded the earth to bring forth
  vegetation
and fruit of every kind.
You provide the sower with seed and give bread
  to eat.
Grant, we pray, that this land,
enriched by your bounty and cultivated by
  human hands,
may be fertile with abundant crops.
Then your people, enriched by the gifts of your
  goodness,
will praise you unceasingly now and for ages
  unending.

Grant this through Christ our Lord.
R. Amen.

*All make the sign of the cross as the leader concludes:*

May God, the source of every good,
bless us and give success to our work,
so that we may receive the joy of his gifts
and praise his name now and for ever.
R. Amen.

*The leader says:*

Let us bless the Lord.

*All respond, making the sign of the cross:*

Thanks be to God.

*The blessing may conclude with song. The
following may be sung to the tune of "All
Creatures of Our God and King."*

Dear mother earth, who day by day
Unfolds rich blessing on our way,
O praise God! Alleluia!
The fruits and flowers that verdant grow,
Let them his praise abundant show.
O praise God, O praise God,
Alleluia, Alleluia, Alleluia.

St. Francis of Assisi

## ASSUMPTION DAY
## BLESSING OF PRODUCE

On August 15, or another appropriate day, the produce of fields, gardens, and orchards may be blessed. Those who take part should assemble in an appropriate place around the grains, fruits, and vegetables to be blessed.

*All make the sign of the cross. The leader begins:*

Let us ever praise and extol God's all-embracing providence, who gives us food from the fruits of the earth. Blessed be God for ever.

*All respond:*

Blessed be God for ever.

*The leader may use these or similar words to introduce the blessing:*

The Lord has bestowed the fruits of the earth for the benefit of all the world's people. May we share with all in need and so be good stewards of God's earth and its abundance. We remember the words Mary speaks in the gospel story of the visitation: "The hungry he has filled with good things."

*Then the Scripture is read:*

Listen to the words of the prophet Joel:

Fear not, O land!
  exult and rejoice!
  for the LORD has done great things.
Fear not, beasts of the field!
  for the pastures of the plain are green;
The tree bears its fruit,
  the fig tree and the vine give their yield.

And do you, O children of Zion,
  exult and rejoice in the LORD, your God!
He has given you the teacher of justice:
  He has made the rain come down for you,
  the early and the late rain as before.
The threshing floors shall be full of grain
  and the vats shall overflow with wine and oil.

You shall eat and be filled,
  and shall praise the name of the LORD, your
  God,
Because he has dealt wondrously with you. . . .
Joel 2:21-24,26

*(The family's Bible may be used for an alternate
reading such as Deuteronomy 28:1-6.)*

*The reader concludes:*

This is the Word of the Lord.

*All respond:*

Thanks be to God.

*After a time of silence, all join in prayers of intercession. The following petitions may be included. On August 15, the Litany of the Blessed Virgin Mary (page 343) may be used.*

That the rights and needs of all may be
recognized and provided:
we pray to the Lord.
That all may be fed and none go hungry:
we pray to the Lord.
That all may have life and have its fullness:
we pray to the Lord.
That we may give thanks not only with our lips
but in our lives:
we pray to the Lord.
That God's will be done on earth as it is in
heaven:
we pray to the Lord.

*After the Lord's Prayer, the leader may invite all to extend their hands in blessing:*

All-powerful God,
we appeal to your tender care
that even as you temper the winds and rains
to nurture the fruits of the earth
you will also send upon them the gentle shower
of your blessing.

Fill the hearts of your people with gratitude,
that from the earth's fertility
the hungry may be filled with good things
and the poor and needy proclaim the glory of
your name.

We ask this through Christ our Lord.
R. Amen.

*All make the sign of the cross as the leader*
*concludes:*

Let us bless God,
for ever let us praise and extol the name
of Father, Son, and Holy Spirit.
R. Amen.

*The blessing may conclude with song, such as*
*"Now Thank We All Our God" (page 291). The*
*following hymn, which may be sung to the tune*
*"AR HYD NOS" ["Day is Done"], is also*
*appropriate:*

For the fruits of this creation,
    Thanks be to God;
For the gifts to ev'ry nation,
    Thanks be to God;
For the plowing, sowing, reaping,
Silent growth while we are sleeping,
Future needs in earth's safe keeping,
    Thanks be to God.

In the just reward of labor,
    God's will is done;
In the help we give our neighbor,
    God's will is done;
In our worldwide task of caring
For the hungry and despairing,
In the harvests we are sharing,
    God's will is done.

                                        F. Pratt Green

# SAINT FRANCIS
# BLESSING OF ANIMALS

On October 4, or another appropriate day, the household may join in the blessing of pets and other animals. The blessing takes place wherever the animals can be gathered. Stories about Saint Francis (Francis and the wolf at Gubbio, for example) could precede the blessing.

*All make the sign of the cross. The leader begins:*

Wonderful are all God's works.
Blessed be the name of the Lord.

*All respond:*

Now and for ever.

*The leader may use these or similar words to introduce the blessing:*

The animals of God's creation inhabit the skies, the earth, and the sea. They share in the ways of human beings. They have a part in our lives. Francis of Assisi recognized this when he called the animals, wild and tame, his brothers and sisters. Remembering Francis' love for these brothers and sisters of ours, we invoke God's blessing on these animals, and we thank God for letting us share the earth with all the creatures.

*Then the Scripture is read:*

Listen to the words of the book of Genesis:

[In the beginning,] God said, "Let the water teem with an abundance of living creatures, and on the earth let birds fly beneath the dome of the sky." And so it happened: God created the great sea monsters and all kinds of swimming creatures with which the water teems, and all kinds of winged birds. God saw how good it was, and God blessed them, saying, "Be fertile, multiply, and fill the water of the seas; and let the birds multiply on the earth." Evening came and morning followed—the fifth day.

Then God said, "Let the earth bring forth all kinds of living creatures: cattle, creeping things, and wild animals of all kinds." And so it happened: God made all kinds of wild animals, all kinds of cattle, and all kinds of creeping things of the earth. God saw how good it was.

Genesis 1:20-25

*(The family's Bible may be used for an alternate reading such as Isaiah 11:6-10.)*

*The reader concludes:*

This is the Word of the Lord.

*All respond:*

Thanks be to God.

*After a time of silence, those present offer prayers of intercession for their animals and for all creatures. After the Lord's Prayer, the leader invites all to hold or place their hands on their animals in blessing:*

O God,
you have done all things wisely;
in your goodness you have made us in your
    image
and given us care over other living things.

Reach out with your right hand
and grant that these animals may serve our needs
and that your bounty in the resources of this life
may move us to seek more confidently
the goal of eternal life.

We ask this through Christ our Lord.
R. Amen.

*All make the sign of the cross as the leader concludes:*

May God, who created the animals of this earth
    as a help to us,
continue to protect and sustain us
with the grace his blessing brings,
now and for ever.
R. Amen.

*The blessing may conclude with a song such as "The Old Hundreth" (Praise God from Whom All Blessings Flow) (page 61).*

## OTHER PRAYERS FOR ANIMALS

O Heavenly Father,
protect and bless all things that have breath.
Guard them from all evil,
and let them sleep in peace.

Albert Schweitzer

Hear our humble prayer, O God,
for our friends the animals, your creatures.
We pray especially for all that are suffering in
    any way:
for the overworked and underfed,
the hunted, lost, or hungry;
for all in captivity or ill-treated,
and for those that must be put to death.

For those who deal with them
we ask a heart of compassion,
    gentle hands, and kindly words.
Make us all true friends to animals
and worthy followers of our merciful Savior,
    Jesus Christ.
R. Amen.

# ALL SAINTS AND ALL SOULS AND NOVEMBER: VISITING A GRAVE

Some or all of the following may be used when visiting the grave of a family member or friend. The month of November, especially All Saints Day and All Souls Day, is a traditional time for visiting graves, as is the anniversary of death. Other appropriate prayers are on page 276 and page 280.

*All make the sign of the cross. The leader begins:*

Praise be to God our Father, who raised Jesus Christ from the dead. Blessed be God for ever.

*All respond:*

Blessed be God for ever.

*One or more of the following Scripture texts may be read:*

We know that if our earthly dwelling, a tent, should be destroyed, we have a building from God, a dwelling not made with hands, eternal in heaven.

2 Corinthians 5:1

I am convinced that neither death, nor life, nor angels, nor principalities, nor present things, nor future things, nor powers, nor height, nor depth, nor any other creature will be able to separate us from the love of God in Christ Jesus our Lord.

Romans 8:38-39

*After a time of silence, all join in prayers of intercession, or in one of the litanies or other prayers (see Part V). All then join hands for the Lord's Prayer.*

*Then the leader prays:*

Lord God,
whose days are without end
and whose mercies beyond counting,
keep us mindful
that life is short and the hour of death unknown.
Let your Spirit guide our days on earth
in the ways of holiness and justice,
that we may serve you
in union with the whole Church,
sure in faith, strong in hope, perfected in love.
And when our earthly journey is ended,
lead us rejoicing into your kingdom,
where you live for ever and ever.
R. Amen.

V. Eternal rest grant unto them, O Lord,
R. and let perpetual light shine upon them.

V. May they rest in peace.
R. Amen.

V. May their souls and the souls of all the
   faithful departed,
   through the mercy of God, rest in peace.
R. Amen.

*All make the sign of the cross as the leader concludes:*

May the peace of God,
which is beyond all understanding,
keep our hearts and minds
in the knowledge and love of God
and of his Son, our Lord Jesus Christ.
R. Amen.

# NOVEMBER PRAYERS

During November, the Church celebrates the communion of saints, intercedes for those who have
died, and prepares to welcome the one Saint Francis
called "Sister Death." These prayers are appropriate
all through November. The Litany of the Saints is
on page 348. Other appropriate prayers are on page
269.

Into your hands, O Lord,
we humbly entrust our brothers and sisters.
In this life you embraced them with your tender
    love;
deliver them now from every evil
and bid them enter eternal rest.

The old order has passed away:
welcome them then into paradise,
where there will be no sorrow, no weeping nor
    pain,
but the fullness of peace and joy
with your Son and the Holy Spirit
for ever and ever.
R. Amen.

O Lord, support us all the day long,
until the shadows lengthen,
and the evening comes,
and the busy world is hushed,
and the fever of life is over,
and our work is done.

Then in your mercy,
grant us a safe lodging,
and a holy rest,
and peace at the last.

John Henry Newman

Bless the LORD, O my soul;
    and all my being, bless his holy name.
Bless the LORD, O my soul,
    and forget not all his benefits.
For as the heavens are high above the earth,
    so surpassing is his kindness toward those who
    fear him.
As far as the east is from the west,
    so far has he put our transgressions from us.
As a father has compassion on his children,
    so the LORD has compassion on those who
    fear him,
For he knows how we are formed;
    he remembers that we are dust.
Man's days are like those of grass;
    like a flower of the field he blooms;
The wind sweeps over him and he is gone,
    and his place knows him no more.
But the kindness of the LORD is from eternity
    to eternity toward those who fear him,
And his justice toward children's children
    among those who keep his covenant
    and remember to fulfill his precepts.

Psalm 103:1-2,11-18

*The following verses may be sung to any appropriate tune such as "The Old Hundreth" (Praise God from Whom All Blessings Flow):*

I know that my Redeemer lives,
And on that final day of days,
His voice shall bid me rise again:
Unending joy, unceasing praise!

This hope I cherish in my heart:
To stand on earth, my flesh restored,
And, not a stranger but a friend,
Behold my Savior and my Lord.

# IMMACULATE CONCEPTION

*On December 8, the Church celebrates this feast of Mary, conceived without sin. She is honored by Catholics in the United States under this title as their patron.*

We praise you, Lord,
in this daughter of Israel,
Mary, your faithful one and our mother.

We pray as she did:
may your name be holy;
may the hungry be filled and the rich know
    hunger;
may the proud be scattered and the oppressed
    raised up;
may your love be ever with your people.

We make our prayer always through Mary's
    child;
he arose from her the sun of justice,
Jesus, who is Lord for ever and ever.
R. Amen.

O Mary, conceived without sin,
pray for us who have recourse to you.

# OUR LADY OF GUADALUPE

*On December 12, the Church celebrates Mary as*
*patron of the Americas: Our Lady of Guadalupe.*
*As one of the poor, Mary spoke for and to the*
*oppressed. In the sufferings of a conquered people,*
*she proclaimed the Church born anew.*

God of power and mercy,
you blessed the Americas at Tepeyac
with the presence of the Virgin Mary of
  Guadalupe.
May her prayers help all men and women
to accept each other as brothers and sisters.
Through your justice present in our hearts
may your peace reign in the world.

Grant this through Christ our Lord.
R. Amen.

# EMBER DAYS

For many centuries, the Church kept three days (Wednesday, Friday, and Saturday) near the beginning of the spring, summer, fall, and winter seasons as times of special penance and intercession. Such ember days echo the meaning and observance of Lent. Ember days are not part of the present calendar, but local Churches may set aside appropriate days for fasting, works of charity, and prayer. Households may wish to observe days (such as those suggested below), which are focused on specific needs in the contemporary world; in this light, see also the prayer for the birthday of Martin Luther King on page 195. The prayers given here may be used within the prayers at table on page 62. The meals themselves would reflect the penitential and vigilant character of these days.

*August 6, August 9.* These are the anniversaries of the atomic bombs dropped on the cities of Hiroshima and Nagasaki. In their pastoral letter *The Challenge of Peace* the bishops of the United States said:

> After the passage of nearly four decades and a concomitant growth in our understanding of the ever growing horror of nuclear war, we must shape the climate of opinion which will make it possible for our country to express profound sorrow over the atomic bombing in 1945. Without that sorrow, there is no possibility of finding a way to repudiate future use of nuclear weapons . . ." (no. 302).

The observance of these two days, in fasting and prayer, would be a way to express this sorrow and to ponder the responsibility for making a peaceful world.


Above the clamor of our violence
your Word of truth resounds,
O God of majesty and power.
Over nations enshrouded in despair
your justice dawns.

Grant your household
a discerning spirit and a watchful eye
to perceive the hour in which we live.
Hasten the advent of that Day
when the weapons of war shall be banished,
our deeds of darkness cast off,
and all your scattered children gathered into one.

We ask this through him whose coming is
    certain,
    whose Day draws near:
your Son, our Lord Jesus Christ,
who lives and reigns with you and the Holy
    Spirit,
one God, for ever and ever.
R. Amen.

*The weekdays before Thanksgiving.* Already the Thanksgiving holiday is associated with special efforts for the hungry and for economic justice. Our consciousness of the great inequality that pervades the world, and of how we are to give thanks in such a world, would grow if these days before Thanksgiving were set aside for deeds of charity, for penance, and for prayers.

A   Almighty God,
    to you belongs the sea, for you made it,
    and the dry land shaped by your hand.
    We hold the riches of the universe only in
    trust.

    Make us honest stewards of your creation,
    careful of the good earth you have given us,
    compassionate and just in sharing its bounty
    with the whole human family.

    We ask this through Christ our Lord.
    R. Amen.

B   God for whom we wait,
    Lord of night and the solemn beauty of
        darkness:
    you have grieved over your creation,
    over our swords and all the terrible weapons
        we fashion.
    Nations and peoples live in fear:
    how can we make tools of our swords
    or take the wages of our weapons to feed the
        hungry?

Give us, Lord, a love that is greater than our
    fear.

We wait for your Messiah,
keeping watch and praying in his name,
Jesus, who is Lord for ever and ever.
R. Amen.


*December 28: Feast of the Holy Innocents.* **The feast
of Christmas is closely bound to this day for
remembering that within the peace of Christmas is the mystery of suffering, even the suffering of the innocent. The household's fasting
and prayer on this day would ponder the ways
the innocent have perished in our own times
through abortion, starvation, and war. Within
the keeping of Christmas, we acknowledge the
sacredness of every human life.**

A   Heavenly Father,
    your holiness revealed in Jesus
    challenges us to renounce violence,
    to forsake revenge,
    and to love without discrimination, without
    measure.

    Teach us the surpassing truth of the Gospel,
    which puts worldly wisdom to shame,
    that we may recognize as one with us
    even our enemies and persecutors
    and see all people as your children.

    We ask this through Christ our Lord.
    R. Amen.

B God our Creator,
   guardian of our homes and source of all
      blessings,
   your Son, begotten before the dawn of
      creation,
   entered the human family
   and was entrusted to the care of Mary and
      Joseph.

   Confirm in us a reverence
   for the gift and mystery of life,
   so that parents and children,
   like the holy family of Nazareth,
   may cherish one another and be heartened by
      your love.

   We ask this through Christ our Lord.
   R. Amen.


*Yom HaShoah.* Twelve days after Passover, many Jewish communities keep a day of remembrance of the six million Jews who perished in the Holocaust. Christians have, at times, joined in this remembrance, facing the ways in which anti-Semitism has been and even now continues to be found among Christians.

A   Exalted, compassionate God,
     grant perfect peace in your sheltering
       Presence,
     among the holy and the pure,
     to the souls of all the men, women, and
       children of the house of Israel,
     to the Righteous Gentiles,
     to the millions who died at a time of madness
       and terror.

     May their memory endure;
     may it inspire truth and loyalty in our lives,
     in our religious commitment, and tasks.
     May their memory be a blessing
       and sign of peace for all humanity.
     And let us say all together: Amen.

B   O God,
     we are conscious that many centuries of
       blindness
     have blinded our eyes
     so that we no longer see the beauty of your
       chosen people,
     nor recognize in their faces the features
       of our privileged brothers and sisters.
     We realize that the mark of Cain stands upon
       our foreheads.
     Across the centuries our brother Abel
     has lain in the blood which we drew
     or which we caused to be shed
     by forgetting your love.
     Forgive us for the curse we falsely attached
       to their name as Jews.
     Forgive us for crucifying you a second time in
       their flesh.

*The following prayer for the Jewish people is appropriate on this day, on Jewish holy days, and at other times:*

God of Abraham and of Moses,
we pray for the Jewish people,
the first to hear your word.
As you have made them your own,
so make them continue to grow in love of your
    name
and in faithfulness to your covenant.
You are our God, living and reigning, for ever
    and ever.
R. Amen.


## PRAYERS AT TABLE ON EMBER DAYS

*See also the prayers on page 62.*


O LORD, hear my prayer,
    and let my cry come to you.
Hide not your face from me
    in the day of my distress.
Incline your ear to me;
    in the day when I call, answer me speedily.
For my days vanish like smoke,
    and my bones burn like fire.
Withered and dried up like grass is my heart;
    I forget to eat my bread.

But you, O LORD, abide forever,
    and your name through all generations.

Psalm 102:2-5,13

# ON FRIDAY

The bishops of the United States, in their pastoral letter *The Challenge of Peace: God's Promise and Our Response*, have asked that Fridays be kept with special observance:

> As a tangible sign of our need and desire to do penance we, for the cause of peace, commit ourselves to fast and abstinence on each Friday of the year. We call upon our people voluntarily to do penance on Friday by eating less food and by abstaining from meat. This return to a traditional practice of penance, once well observed in the U.S. Church, should be accompanied by works of charity and service toward our neighbors. Every Friday should be a day significantly devoted to prayer, penance, and almsgiving for peace (no. 298).

*The following could be read as part of morning prayer on Friday, or at table.*

Listen to the words of the prophet Isaiah:

This, rather, is the fasting that I wish:
   releasing those bound unjustly,
   untying the thongs of the yoke;
Setting free the oppressed,
   breaking every yoke;
Sharing your bread with the hungry,
   sheltering the oppressed and the homeless;
Clothing the naked when you see them,
   and not turning your back on your own.

If you remove from your midst oppression,
    false accusation and malicious speech;
If you bestow your bread on the hungry
    and satisfy the afflicted;
Then light shall rise for you in the darkness,
    and the gloom shall become for you like
    midday.

Isaiah 58:6-7,9-10

*After a brief silence, the leader recites the prayer
"All praise be yours" on page 63.*

*See also the prayer "Lord, make me an instrument
of your peace" on page 124.*

# NATIONAL DAYS

The following prayers may be used as part of the table blessing on the days indicated.

### Martin Luther King's Birthday
(January 15, observed on the third Monday in January)

Lord our God,
see how oppression and violence are our sad
    inheritance,
one generation to the next.
We look for you where the lowly are raised up,
where the mighty are brought down.
We find you there in your servants,
and we give you thanks this day
for your preacher and witness, Martin Luther
    King, Jr.
Fill us with your spirit:
where our human community is divided by
    racism,
torn by repression,
saddened by fear and ignorance,
may we give ourselves to your work of healing.

Grant this through Christ our Lord.
R. Amen.

### George Washington's Birthday
(February 22, observed on the third Monday
in February)

Almighty and eternal God,
you have revealed your glory to all nations.
God of power and might, wisdom and justice,
through you authority is rightly administered,
laws are enacted, and judgment is decreed.

Assist with your spirit of counsel and fortitude
the President of these United States,
that his/her administration
   may be conducted in righteousness,
and be eminently useful to your people
   over whom he/she presides.
May he/she encourage due respect for virtue and
   religion.
May he/she execute the laws with justice and
   mercy.
May he/she seek to restrain crime, vice, and
   immorality.

We, likewise, commend to your unbounded
   mercy
all who dwell in the United States.
Bless us and all people with the peace
which the world cannot give.

We pray to you, who are Lord and God, for ever
   and ever.
R. Amen.

Archbishop John Carroll (alt.)

**Mother's Day**
(Second Sunday in May)

The following prayer may be used with the table blessing. All may stretch out their hands over the mother in a gesture of blessing.

May God,
the source of life,
give you joy in the love, growth,
and holiness of your children.
R. Amen.

*The following prayer may also be appropriate:*

Loving God,
as a mother gives life and nourishment to her
    children,
so you watch over your Church.
Bless our mother.
Let the example of her faith and love shine forth.
Grant that we, her family,
may honor her always
with a spirit of profound respect.

Grant this through Christ our Lord.
R. Amen.

### Memorial Day
(Last Monday in May)

*The following intercessory prayer may be prayed:*

For those who suffer most from war: that the homeless, the orphaned, the hungry, and the innocent may challenge us to turn from warlike ways and accept God's gift of peace, we pray to the Lord.
R. Lord, hear our prayer.

V. Eternal rest grant unto them, O Lord.
R. And let perpetual light shine upon them.

V. May they rest in peace.
R. Amen.

*See also the prayers for November on page 181.*

### Father's Day
(Third Sunday in June)

The following prayer may be used with the table blessing. All may stretch out their hands over the father in a gesture of blessing.

May God, who gives life on earth and in heaven, lead you to walk by the light of faith
and so help your children attain the good things Christ has promised us.
R. Amen.

*The following prayer may also be appropriate:*

God our Father,
in your wisdom and love you made all things.
Bless our father.
Let the example of his faith and love shine forth.
Grant that we, his family,
may honor him always
with a spirit of profound respect.

Grant this through Christ our Lord.
R. Amen.


**Independence Day**
(July 4)

God, source of all freedom,
this day is bright with the memory
of those who declared that life and liberty
are your gift to every human being.

Help us to continue a good work begun long ago.
Make our vision clear and our will strong:
that only in human solidarity will we find liberty,
and justice only in the honor that belongs
to every life on earth.

Turn our hearts toward the family of nations:
to understand the ways of others,
to offer friendship,
and to find safety only in the common good of
  all.

We ask this through Christ our Lord.
R. Amen.

**Labor Day**
(First Monday in September)

God our creator,
we are the work of your hands.
Guide us in our work,
that we may do it, not for self alone,
but for the common good.
Make us alert to injustice,
ready to stand in solidarity,
that there may be dignity for all
in labor and in labor's reward.

Grant this through Christ our Lord.
R. Amen.

V. Joseph, patron of laborers,
R. pray for us.

**Thanksgiving Day**
(Fourth Thursday in November)

*When all have gathered at table, the following
prayer and song may be used. One of the blessings
of the table on page 50 may be added. The prayer
may begin with a scripture reading (Philippians
4:4-7, page 310, for example).*

Lord, we thank you
for the goodness of our people
and for the spirit of justice
that fills this nation.
We thank you for the beauty and fullness of the
land and the challenge of the cities.

We thank you for our work and our rest,
for one another, and for our homes.
We thank you, Lord:

*(Pause for other prayers of thanksgiving.)*

For all that we have spoken
and for all that we keep in our hearts,
accept our thanksgiving on this day.

We pray and give thanks through Jesus Christ
our Lord.
R. Amen.

*"Now Thank We All Our God," (page 291); "Holy
God, We Praise Thy Name" (page 333); or
another song may then be sung.*

PART III
TIMES IN LIFE
BLESSINGS OF FAMILY
MEMBERS

# INTRODUCTION

Peoples of all times and places have made special those moments when the life of the individual and the household undergoes change. These are the times of passage. Within them, we seek God's blessing. Around the birth of a child, at turning points in the child's life, at marriage, in the lifelong journey to reconciliation, during sickness, at death: here we know our need for one another, our need for God's protection, and here we know also the wonder of God's grace and the strength of our family and community.

At many of these moments, the Church's ministers are present. The rites that the Church celebrates at such times are echoed in the brief prayers and blessings found on these pages. Parents and other members of the household should become familiar with the content of the rites. Most of them will not be used often, but they bring faith and wholeness to the great and small turning points in the family's life.

# BLESSING FOR
# A FAMILY OR HOUSEHOLD

This rite may be used annually on a day of special significance to a family, or at times when members of the family who live far apart have come together, or at times when the family experiences special difficulties or special joys. The leader may be someone from outside the family (a priest, deacon, or lay minister) or may be one of the family members. The blessing may be given at a family meal or another appropriate time.

*All make the sign of the cross. The leader begins:*

The grace of our Lord Jesus Christ be with us all, now and for ever.
R. Amen.

*The leader may use these words or words directed to the specific occasion to introduce the blessing:*

We are a family. For one another, we are love and trial, strength and trouble. Even when far apart, we belong to one another and, in various ways, we remember and pray for one another. We join now to give thanks to our God and to ask God's blessing on this family (those who are present and those who are not here).

*Then the Scripture is read:*

Listen to the words of the apostle Paul to the Colossians:

Put on then, as God's chosen ones, holy and beloved, heartfelt compassion, kindness, humility, gentleness, and patience, bearing with one another and forgiving one another, if one has a grievance against another; as the Lord has forgiven you, so must you also do. And over all these put on love, that is, the bond of perfection. And let the peace of Christ control your hearts, the peace into which you were also called in one body. And be thankful. Let the word of Christ dwell in you richly, as in all wisdom you teach and admonish one another, singing psalms, hymns, and spiritual songs with gratitude in your hearts to God. And whatever you do, in word or

in deed, do everything in the name of the Lord
Jesus, giving thanks to God the Father through
him.

Colossians 3:12-17

*(The family's Bible may be used for an alternate
reading such as Ephesians 4:1-6 or 1 Corinthians
12:31—13:7.)*

*The reader concludes:*

This is the Word of the Lord.

*All respond:*

Thanks be to God.

*After a time of silence, all offer prayers of
intercession, remembering especially those who
have died. Then all join hands for the Lord's
Prayer.*

*The leader says the prayer of blessing:*

A  O God,
    you have created us in love and saved us in
      mercy,
    and through the bond of marriage
    you have established the family
    and willed that it should become a sign
      of Christ's love for his Church.

    Shower your blessings on this family
      gathered here in your name.

Enable those who are joined by one love
to support one another
by their fervor of spirit and devotion to
    prayer.
Make them responsive to the needs of others
and witnesses to the faith in all they say and
    do.

We ask this through Christ our Lord.
R. Amen.

Or:

**B** In good times and in bad,
in sickness and in health,
we belong to each other
as we belong to you, God ever faithful.
By morning and by night
may your name be on our lips,
a blessing to all our days:
so may kindness and patience be ever among
    us,
a hunger for justice,
and songs of thankfulness in all we do.

We ask this through Christ our Lord.
R. Amen.

*The leader may sprinkle all with holy water, or
each one may take holy water and make the sign of
the cross.*

*The leader concludes:*

May the Lord Jesus,
who lived with his holy family in Nazareth,
dwell also with your (our) family,
keep it from all evil,
and make all of you (us) one in heart and mind.
R. Amen.

*The leader says:*

Let us bless the Lord.

*All respond, making the sign of the cross:*

Thanks be to God.

*The blessing may conclude with singing "Now Thank We All Our God," (page 291) or another appropriate song.*

# BLESSING ON BIRTHDAYS
# OR THE ANNIVERSARY
# OF BAPTISM

A member of the household may lead this prayer
at table or at another time. A reading from Scripture
may be selected and read before one of the following
prayers.


God of all creation,
we offer you grateful praise for the gift of life.
Hear the prayers of N., your servant,
who recalls today the gift of his/her birth/baptism
and rejoices in your gifts of life and love,
    family and friends.

Bless him/her with your presence
and surround him/her with your love
that he/she may enjoy many happy years,
all of them pleasing to you.

We ask this through Christ our Lord.
R. Amen.

*Or, on the anniversary of baptism:*

A   God of the covenant,
     you anointed your beloved Son
     with the power of the Holy Spirit
     to be light for the nations
     and release for captives.

     May N., who has been born again
     of water and the Spirit,
     proclaim with his/her lips the good news of
       peace
     and manifest in his/her life the victory of
       justice.

We ask this through Christ our Lord.
R. Amen.

B   Remember this, N.
     You have been washed
     in the saving waters of baptism
     and anointed with holy oil.
     Place on your head and in your heart
     the sign of the cross of salvation.

*Or, for children:*

Loving God,
you created all the people of the world,
and you know each of us by name.
We thank you for N.,
who celebrates his/her birthday/anniversary of
　baptism.
Bless him/her with your love and friendship
that he/she may grow in wisdom, knowledge,
　and grace.
May he/she love his/her family always
and be ever faithful to his/her friends.

Grant this through Christ our Lord.
R. Amen.

> *Those present may place their hands on the head
> or shoulders of the one being blessed.*

May God, in whose presence our ancestors
walked, bless you.
R. Amen.
May God, who has been your shepherd from
birth until now, keep you.
R. Amen.
May God, who saves you from all harm, give you
peace.
R. Amen.

*The blessing may include a song:*

O God, our help in ages past,
Our hope for years to come,
Our shelter from the stormy blast,
And our eternal home.

Before the hills in order stood,
Or earth received its frame,
From everlasting you are God,
To endless years the same.

Isaac Watts

# BLESSINGS BEFORE AND AFTER BIRTH

## BLESSING FOR THE CONCEPTION OR ADOPTION OF A CHILD

For couples who hope to conceive or adopt a child, this psalm and prayer can be joined to table prayers or used at other times.

The LORD is faithful in all his words
    and holy in all his works.
The LORD lifts up all who are falling
    and raises up all who are bowed down.

The eyes of all look hopefully to you,
  and you give them their food in due season;
You open your hand
  and satisfy the desire of every living thing.

The LORD is just in all his ways
  and holy in all his works.
The LORD is near to all who call upon him,
  to all who call upon him in truth.
He fulfills the desire of those who fear him,
  he hears their cry and saves them.
The LORD keeps all who love him,
  but all the wicked he will destroy.

May my mouth speak the praise of the LORD,
and may all flesh bless his holy name forever and
  ever.

Psalm 145:13-21

God our creator,
by your love the world is filled with life,
through your generosity one generation
  gives life to another,
and so are your wonders told and your praises
  sung.

We look to you in our love and in our need:
may it be your will that we bear (adopt) a child
to share our home and faith.

Loving God, be close to us
as we pray to love and do your will.
You are our God, nourishing us for ever and
  ever.
R. Amen.

# BLESSING DURING PREGNANCY FOR BOTH PARENTS

When a pregnancy is first confirmed and at various times during the pregnancy (when the extended family is present, for example), this blessing is appropriate. It may simply take place as part of the blessing at table, using the scripture reading and prayer of blessing before joining in the grace for meals. A blessing of the mother only, page 220, may be used when it is more appropriate. The leader may be a priest, deacon, lay minister, a friend, or member of the family.

*All make the sign of the cross. The leader begins:*

Blessed be God for ever.

*All respond:*

Blessed be God for ever.

*The leader may use these or similar words to introduce the blessing:*

As you await your child's birth in faith, partners in God's own love, may you already cherish the child you have conceived.

*Then the Scripture is read:*

Listen to the words of the holy gospel according to Luke:

During those days Mary set out and traveled to the hill country in haste to a town of Judah, where she entered the house of Zechariah and greeted Elizabeth. When Elizabeth heard Mary's greeting, the infant leapt in her womb, and Elizabeth, filled with the holy Spirit, cried out in a loud voice and said, "Most blessed are you among women, and blessed is the fruit of your womb. And how does this happen to me, that the mother of my Lord should come to me? For at the moment the sound of your greeting reached my ears, the infant in my womb leapt for joy. Blessed are you who believed that what was spoken to you by the Lord would be fulfilled."

Luke 1:39-45

*The reader concludes:*

This is the Gospel of the Lord.

*All respond:*

Praise to you, Lord Jesus Christ.

*After a time of silence, all join in prayers of intercession. The Hail Mary, the Memorare, or other prayers for the protection of Mary (page 362) may be appropriate. After the Lord's Prayer, the leader may invite all to extend their hands toward the parents or to place their hands in blessing on the parents.*

Gracious Father,
your Word, spoken in love, created the human
    family
and your Son, conceived in love,
    restored it to your friendship.

Hear the prayers of N. and N.,
who await the birth of their child.
Calm their fears when they are anxious.

Watch over and support these parents
and bring their child into this world
safely and in good health,
so that as members of your family
they may praise you and glorify you
through your Son, our Lord Jesus Christ,
now and for ever.
R. Amen.

> *All make the sign of the cross. The leader
> concludes:*

May God, who chose to make known and to
    send
the blessings of eternal salvation
through the motherhood of the Blessed Virgin
    Mary
and the protection of Saint Joseph,
bless us and keep us in his care,
now and for ever.
R. Amen.

# BLESSING DURING PREGNANCY FOR THE MOTHER

When a pregnancy is first confirmed and at various times during the pregnancy (when the extended family is present, for example), this blessing is appropriate (but see also the blessing of both parents on page 217). It may simply take place as part of the blessing at table, using the scripture reading and prayer of blessing for the mother before joining in the grace for meals. The leader may be a priest, deacon, lay minister, a friend, or a member of the family.

*All make the sign of the cross. The leader begins:*

Let us bless the Lord Jesus, who in the womb of the Virgin Mary became one of us. Blessed be God for ever.

*All respond:*

Blessed be God for ever.

*The leader may use these or similar words to introduce the blessing:*

Join now in listening to the Scripture and in blessing this mother-to-be that she may cherish the child in her womb and await birth with great hope and faith.

*Then the Scripture is read:*

Listen to the words of the holy gospel according to Luke:

During those days Mary set out and traveled to the hill country in haste to a town of Judah, where she entered the house of Zechariah and greeted Elizabeth. When Elizabeth heard Mary's greeting, the infant leapt in her womb, and Elizabeth, filled with the holy Spirit, cried out in a loud voice and said, "Most blessed are you among women, and blessed is the fruit of your womb. And how does this happen to me, that the mother of my Lord should come to me? For at the moment the sound of your greeting reached my ears, the infant in my womb leapt for joy. Blessed are you who believed that what was spoken to you by the Lord would be fulfilled."

Luke 1:39-45

*The reader concludes:*

This is the Gospel of the Lord.

*All respond:*

Praise to you, Lord Jesus Christ.

*After a time of silence, all join in prayers of intercession. The Hail Mary, the Memorare, or other prayers for the protection of Mary (page 362) may be appropriate. After the Lord's Prayer, the leader may invite all to extend their hands toward the mother or place their hands on her in blessing.*

A   Gracious Father,
    your Word, spoken in love, created the
        human family
    and your Son, conceived in love,
        restored it to your friendship.

    Hear the prayers of N.,
    who awaits the birth of her child.
    Calm her fears when she is anxious.

    Watch over and support her
    and bring her child into this world
    safely and in good health,
    so that as members of your family
    she and her child may praise you and glorify
        you
    through your Son, our Lord Jesus Christ,
    now and for ever.
    R. Amen.

Or:

B   God has brought gladness and light to the
        world
    through the Virgin Mary's delivery of her
        child.
    May Christ fill your heart with his holy joy
    and keep you and your baby safe from harm.
    We ask this in his name, who is Lord,
    for ever and ever.
    R. Amen.

    *All make the sign of the cross as the leader
    concludes:*

May God, who chose to make known and to
    send
the blessings of eternal salvation
through the motherhood of the Blessed Virgin,
bless us and keep us in his care,
now and for ever.
R. Amen.


# BLESSING NEAR THE TIME OF BIRTH

*Blessing of the Mother:*

Loving God,
your love for us is like that of a mother
and you know the hard joy of giving birth.

Hold the hand of your servant N. now and keep
    her safe;
put your own spirit into her very breathing
and into the new baby,
for whom we wait with awe and hope.

We ask this through Christ our Lord.
R. Amen.


*Prayer of the Mother:*

Lord God,
you made us out of nothing
and redeemed us by the precious blood of your
    only Son.

Preserve the work of your hands,
and defend both me and the tender fruit of my
   womb
from all perils and evils.
I beg of you, for myself,
your grace, protection, and a happy delivery.
Sanctify my child
any make this child yours for ever.

Grant this through Christ our Lord.
R. Amen.

## THANKSGIVING FOR A NEWBORN OR NEWLY ADOPTED CHILD

On first holding a newborn or newly adopted child, on bringing the child into the home for the first time, and on other occasions before the child's baptism, this blessing may be given by the parents.

A   God, our creator, cherish this child.
     Jesus, our savior, protect him/her.
     Holy Spirit, our comforter, strengthen him/her.

Or:

B   Source of all blessings, Protector of infants, look with favor on this child, N.

Hold him/her gently in your hands.
When he/she is reborn of water and the
    Holy Spirit,
bring him/her into the Church,
there to share in your kingdom
and with us to bless your name for ever.

We ask this through Christ our Lord.
R. Amen.

*The parents trace the sign of the cross on the
child's forehead.*

N. may the Lord Jesus, who loved children,
bless you and keep you in his love,
now and for ever.
R. Amen.


## PARENTS' THANKSGIVING

O God, we give you thanks for N.
whom you have welcomed into our family.
Bless this family.

Confirm a lively sense of your presence with us,
and grant us patience and wisdom,
that our lives may show forth the love of Christ,
as we bring N. up to love all that is good.

We ask this through Christ our Lord.
R. Amen.

# BLESSING ON BRINGING
# A CHILD INTO THE HOME

Good Lord,
you have tenderly loved us,
and given us this home and good friends.

May we make a true home for this child
where he/she will learn trust in us and in you.
(May his/her brothers and sisters rejoice
  in their own growing up
as they help to care for this child.)

We ask this through Christ our Lord.
R. Amen.


# MOTHER'S BLESSING OF THE CHILD
# WHEN NURSING OR FEEDING

God,
you are like a mother to us all,
nourishing all creatures with food and with
  blessing.
Strengthen my child with (my milk, this food)
and with the warmth of our nearness.

Or:

Blessed are you, Lord, God of all creation:
you nourish all your children.

# BLESSINGS DURING CHILDHOOD

## DAILY BLESSING OF A CHILD

One of the following short blessings may be said by the parent at various times, such as when a child is going to play or to school, but especially when the child is going to bed each night. Other night prayers are on page 90 . The parent makes the sign of the cross on the child's forehead or heart and says one of the following blessings.

May God bless you.

May God keep you safe.

God be with you.

God be in your heart.

May God bless and protect you.

# BLESSING FOR SPECIAL OCCASIONS

The following are scripture texts and prayers of blessing appropriate for the occasion mentioned. They may often be used as part of the blessing at table when the family gathers to celebrate the event. During the blessing, those present place their hands over or on the one being blessed.

### BLESSING ON A BIRTHDAY

The Lord said to Jeremiah:
Before I formed you in the womb I knew you,
before you were born I dedicated you.

Jeremiah 1:5

May God, in whose presence our ancestors
walked, bless you.
R. Amen.
May God, who has been your shepherd from
birth until now, keep you.
R. Amen.
May God, who saves you from all harm, give you
peace.
R. Amen.

## BLESSING ON A NAME'S DAY

On the feast of the saint for whom a child is named, the following blessing may be used. The life of the saint may also be related.

God of glory,
whom we name in many ways,
when we brought this child to your Church
we were asked, "What name do you give this
    child?"
We answered, "N" (or: "N. N."),
and so our child was claimed for Christ by that
    name.

May Saint N. ever pray for him/her,
may he/she guard him/her
so that N. might overcome all evil
and come at last to that place
where his/her name is written in the book of life.

We ask this through Christ our Lord.
R. Amen.

## BLESSING ON THE ANNIVERSARY OF BAPTISM

On this day, or yearly on Easter Sunday, the baptismal garment may be displayed, the baptismal candle lighted, and holy water placed in a bowl. In some years, the renewal of baptismal vows may be appropriate (see page 371).

N., on this day the Christian community
  welcomed you with great joy.
You were baptized in the name of the Father,
  and of the Son, and of the Holy Spirit.
You put on the Lord Jesus.
Today we sign you again with the cross
  by which you were claimed for Christ,
and we pray that God's blessing be upon you.

*Each person signs the forehead of the one
celebrating the anniversary and says:*

Blessed be God who chose you in Christ.

*In conclusion, all may sign themselves with holy
water, saying:*

In the name of the Father, and of the Son, and of
  the Holy Spirit.
R. Amen.


## BLESSING BEFORE CONFIRMATION

During the months when a candidate is preparing
for confirmation, and especially on the day of the
celebration, parents and sponsors may bless the
candidate.


N., in baptism you were claimed for Christ.
May God bless you now and watch over you.

## BLESSING BEFORE FIRST COMMUNION

During the months when a child is preparing for first holy communion, and especially as the day approaches, parents may bless the candidate.

N., may the Lord Jesus touch your ears to receive
  his word,
and your mouth to proclaim his faith.
May you come with joy to his supper
to the praise and glory of God.
R. Amen.

# GODPARENT'S BLESSING OF A CHILD

At baptism, godparents promise to help parents in their duties as Christian mothers and fathers. Throughout the years of childhood it is appropriate for a godparent to bless his/her godchild, perhaps with a cross traced on the child's forehead. One of the following short blessings may be prayed:

N., blessed be God who chose you in Christ.

N., may Christ's peace reign in your heart.

# BLESSING FOR TIMES OF SICKNESS

When a child is ill, parents and others may bless him/her. When the illness is more serious, the parish priest should be asked to visit and to join the family in prayer and perhaps in the anointing of the sick (page 261). A longer blessing of the sick will be found on page 252.

*When the parents wish to give a simple blessing, they may place a hand on the child's head and say one of the following prayers:*

A  God of love,
    ever caring, ever strong,
    stand by us in our time of need.

    Watch over N., who is sick;
    look after him/her in every danger,
    and grant him/her your healing and peace.

    We ask this in the name of Jesus the Lord.
    R. Amen.

B  N., when you were baptized,
    you were marked with the cross of Jesus.
    I (we) make this cross + on your forehead
    and ask the Lord to bless you
    and restore you to health.
    R. Amen.

C  May the Lord Jesus watch over you
    and keep you in peace.
    R. Amen.

# BLESSING FOR TIMES OF TROUBLE

When there is difficulty in the life of the family or one of its members, one of the following blessings may be prayed at table or at bedside. At times, parents may pray these prayers silently for an older child.

A  Praised be God, the Father of our Lord
      Jesus Christ,
    the Father of mercies and the God of all
      consolation,
    who comforts us in all our afflictions.

B  May God, the source of all patience and
      encouragement,
    enable us to live in perfect harmony with one
      another
    according to the spirit of Christ Jesus.
    R. Amen.

C  May the Lord make us overflow with love for
      one another and for all.
    May God strengthen our hearts.
    R. Amen.

D  God of all our days:
    like a parent you forgive us,
    and like a child you love us.
    May we love and forgive one another.

## BLESSING FOR TIMES OF NEW BEGINNINGS

When a child is ready to begin school or for some other new undertaking, the parents may bless the child by placing a hand on the child's head and saying:

May the Lord bless you and keep you.
R. Amen.

May the Lord's face shine upon you,
and be gracious to you.
R. Amen.

May the Lord look upon you with kindness,
and give you peace.
R. Amen.

## BLESSING FOR SAFETY

Strong and faithful God,
keep our son/daughter safe from injury and harm
and make him/her a blessing to all he/she meets
today.
R. Amen.

# BLESSING FOR STRENGTH

God,
we pray for our young people,
growing up in an unsteady and confusing world.

Show them that your ways give more life
   than the ways of the world,
and that following you is better
   than chasing after selfish goals.

Help them to take failure,
not as a measure of their worth,
but as a chance for a new start.

Give them strength to hold their faith in you,
and to keep alive their joy in your creation.

We ask this through Christ our Lord.
R. Amen.

# BLESSINGS RELATED TO MARRIAGE

## BLESSING OF AN ENGAGED COUPLE

Ordinarily, the blessing of an engaged couple is celebrated by both families, perhaps at a meal together.

*All make the sign of the cross. One of the parents begins:*

Brothers and sisters,
let us praise our Lord Jesus Christ,
who loved us and gave himself for us.
Let us bless him now and for ever.

Blessed be God for ever.

*The leader may use these or similar words to introduce the blessing:*

We know that all of us need God's blessing at all times; but at the time of their engagement to be married, Christians are in particular need of grace as they prepare themselves to form a new family. Let us pray, then, for God's blessing to come upon this couple, our brother and sister: that as they await the day of their wedding, they will grow in mutual respect and in their love for one another; that through their companionship and prayer together they will prepare themselves rightly and chastely for marriage.

*Then the Scripture is read:*

Listen to the words of the apostle Paul to the Corinthians:

Love is patient, love is kind. It is not jealous, [love] is not pompous, it is not inflated, it is not rude, it does not seek its own interests, it is not quick-tempered, it does not brood over injury, it does not rejoice over wrongdoing but rejoices with the truth. It bears all things, believes all things, hopes all things, endures all things.

Love never fails. If there are prophecies, they will be brought to nothing; if tongues, they will cease; if knowledge, it will be brought to nothing. For we know partially and we prophesy partially, but when the perfect comes, the partial will pass away. When I was a child, I used to talk as a child, think as a child, reason as a child; when I became a man, I put aside childish things. At present we see indistinctly, as in a mirror, but then face to face. At present I know partially; then I shall know fully, as I am fully known. So faith, hope, love remain, these three; but the greatest of these is love.

1 Corinthians 13:4-13

*(The family's Bible may be used for an alternate reading such as John 15:9-12.)*

*The reader concludes:*

This is the Word of the Lord.

*All respond:*

Thanks be to God.

*After a time of silence, all join in prayers of intercession for the couple and for others. All recite the Lord's Prayer. Then the engaged couple may exchange rings or some other gift that signifies their pledge to each other. One of the parents may bless these gifts:*

N. and N., in due course may you honor the
sacred pledge symbolized by these gifts which
you now exchange.
R. Amen.

> *Parents may then place their hands on their
> children's heads in blessing. One or more of the
> parents speaks the blessing:*

We praise you, Lord,
for your gentle plan draws together
   your children, N. and N.,
in love for one another.
Strengthen their hearts,
so that they will keep faith with each other,
please you in all things,
and so come to the happiness of celebrating
   the sacrament of their marriage.

We ask this through Christ our Lord.
R. Amen.

> *All make the sign of the cross as the leader
> concludes:*

May the God of love and peace
abide in you, guide your steps,
and confirm your hearts in his love,
now and for ever.
R. Amen.

> *The blessing may conclude with song. The
> following may be sung to a tune such as "The Old
> Hundreth" (Praise God from Whom All Blessings
> Flow).*

From all that dwell below the skies,
Let the Creator's praise arise;
Let the Redeemer's name be sung,
Through ev'ry land by ev'ry tongue.

In ev'ry land begin the song;
To ev'ry land the strains belong;
In cheerful sounds all voices raise,
And fill the world with loudest praise.

Isaac Watts

## BLESSING OF A SON OR DAUGHTER BEFORE MARRIAGE

Before the wedding, the family may gather around its member who is to be married, perhaps at a special meal in the family's home.

*All make the sign of the cross. A parent begins:*

Let us bless the Lord,
by whose goodness we live
and by whose grace we love one another.
Blessed be God for ever.

*All respond:*

Blessed be God for ever.

*Then the Scripture is read:*

Listen to the words of the book of Deuteronomy:

Hear, O Israel! The LORD is our God, the LORD alone! Therefore, you shall love the LORD, your God, with all your heart, and with all your soul, and with all your strength. Take to heart these words which I enjoin on you today. Drill them into your children. Speak of them at home and abroad, whether you are busy or at rest.

Deuteronomy 6:4-7

*The reader concludes:*

This is the Word of the Lord.

*All respond:*

Thanks be to God.

*The parents may give a Bible to the one who is to be married. Then all join in prayers of intercession for the couple to be married and for the world. After the Lord's Prayer, the parents and other family members place their hands on the head of their son/daughter as one parent speaks the blessing.*

May the Lord, who gave you into our care
and made you a joy to our home,
bless you and keep you.
R. Amen.

May the Lord, who turns the hearts of parents to
    their children
and the hearts of children to their parents,
smile on you and be kind to you.
R. Amen.

May the Lord, who delights in our love for one
   another,
turn toward you and give you peace.
R. Amen.

*All make the sign of the cross as the leader
concludes:*

May the God of love and peace
abide in you, guide your steps,
and confirm your heart in his love,
now and for ever.
R. Amen.

## BLESSING IN TIMES OF TROUBLE

Some of the following texts may be used at times
when the family faces great difficulties, whether
these be from outside (unemployment, prejudice,
uncertainty, and fear, for example) or from within.
See also prayers for times of suffering and need
(page 311) and prayers for times of penance and
reconciliation (page 315) and prayers for the help
of Mary (page 362).

*The following blessing may be used at table or at
bedside; prayers of intercession and the Lord's
Prayer may be added.*

I lift my eyes toward the mountains;
   whence shall help come to me?
My help is from the LORD,
   who made heaven and earth.

May he not suffer your foot to slip;
  may he slumber not who guards you:
Indeed he neither slumbers nor sleeps,
  the guardian of Israel.

The LORD is your guardian; the LORD is your
  shade;
  he is beside you at your right hand.
The sun shall not harm you by day,
  nor the moon by night.

The LORD will guard you from all evil;
  he will guard your life.
The LORD will guard your coming and your
  going,
  both now and forever.

Psalm 121

Most holy and most merciful God,
strength of the weak,
rest of the weary,
comfort of the sorrowful,
savior of the sinful,
our refuge in every time of need:
grant us strength and protect us;
support us in all dangers,
and carry us through all trials.

Grant this through Christ our Lord.
R. Amen.

May the God of hope help us to be tolerant of
   one another,
following the example of Jesus Christ,
so that one in mind and voice
we may give glory to God.


## BLESSING ON ANNIVERSARIES

With family and friends, or alone, a couple may
keep their wedding anniversary with prayer for
God's blessing. Other Scriptures may be chosen as
appropriate.

*All make the sign of the cross as they say:*

Blessed be the God of all consolation,
who has shown us his great mercy.
Blessed be God now and for ever.

*All respond:*

Blessed be God for ever.

*Then the Scripture is read:*

Listen to the words of the apostle Paul to the
Corinthians:

Love is patient, love is kind. It is not jealous,
[love] is not pompous, it is not inflated, it is not
rude, it does not seek its own interests, it is not

quick-tempered, it does not brood over injury, it does not rejoice over wrongdoing but rejoices with the truth. It bears all things, believes all things, hopes all things, endures all things. Love never fails.

1 Corinthians 13:4-8

*The reader concludes:*

This is the Word of the Lord.

*All respond:*

Thanks be to God.

> *After a time of silence, all join in prayers of intercession and in the Lord's Prayer. If no one else is present, the couple prays form A of the blessing prayer. Otherwise, form B is read by a family member or friend.*

A   Almighty and eternal God,
you have so exalted the unbreakable bond of
   marriage
that it has become the sacramental sign
of your Son's union with the Church as his
   spouse.

Look with favor on us whom you have
   united in marriage,
as we ask for your help
and the protection of the Virgin Mary.
We pray that in good times and in bad
we will grow in love for each other;
that we will resolve to be of one heart
in the bond of peace.

Lord, in our struggles let us rejoice
that you are near to help us;
in our needs let us know
that you are there to rescue us;
in our joys let us see
that you are the source and completion of
   every happiness.

We ask this through Christ our Lord.
R. Amen.

B   Almighty and eternal God,
    you have so exalted the unbreakable bond of
       marriage
    that it has become the sacramental sign
    of your Son's union with the Church as his
       spouse.

    Look with favor on N. and N.,
    whom you have united in marriage
    as they ask for your help
    and the protection of the Virgin Mary.
    They pray that in good times and in bad
    they will grow in love for each other;
    that they will resolve to be of one heart
    in the bond of peace.

    Lord, in their struggles let them rejoice
    that you are near to help them;
    in their needs let them know
    that you are there to rescue them;
    in their joys let them see
    that you are the source and completion of
       every happiness.

We ask this through Christ our Lord.
R. Amen.

*If they wish to do so, the couple may renew the vows of marriage. Each one says:*

I, N., take you, N., to be my wife/husband. I promise to be true to you in good times and in bad, in sickness and in health. I will love you and honor you all the days of my life.

*All make the sign of the cross as they conclude:*

May the God of hope fill us with every joy in
   believing.
May the peace of Christ abound in our hearts.
May the Holy Spirit enrich us with his gifts,
now and for ever.
R. Amen.

# PENANCE AND RECONCILIATION

The evil we do to one another and the ways we fail to do good are ever present in our lives and prayer. Daily in the Lord's Prayer, the Christian asks for forgiveness and prays for deliverance from evil. Each night, there is the prayer of confession and contrition and the petition addressed to Mary: "Pray for us, sinners." We begin the Sunday eucharist by praising God for a mercy that is greater than our sins. Friday has been a day traditionally set aside for fasting and deeds of charity so that we might turn our lives to the way of the gospel. Each year, Christians keep the season of Lent: forty days for finding anew the strength to renounce evil, to profess Christ as our Lord, and so to live again in the grace of baptism.

Repentance and reconciliation are thus constant and lifelong. Some moments in each person's life are marked with the sacrament that bears this name of penance and reconciliation. Even something as personal as sin, as personal as sorrow and confession, is brought to the community, to the Church, and the Church's ministers. The Church comes together—even if only the penitent and the priest— so that God's pardon may be sought in the confession of sin, sorrow, deeds of penance, and the expression of God's forgiveness in words of absolution. The sacrament embraces all these moments. It springs from the Church's faith that, though sin is personal, it is not private: "Penance always entails reconciliation with our brothers and sisters who are always harmed by our sins" (*Rite of Penance*, no. 5).

When the sacrament of penance is celebrated with a number of persons present, the rite begins with the reading of Scripture and includes a homily, examination of conscience, individual confession and absolution, praise of God's mercy, and prayers of thanksgiving. When an individual comes alone for the sacrament of penance, the order below is observed. Prayers for times of penance and reconciliation in the household are on page 315. See also the prayer for Fridays on page 193, and the lenten prayers on pages 132 and 137.

*After a greeting, the priest and penitent make the sign of the cross together:*

In the name of the Father, and of the Son, and of the Holy Spirit. Amen.

*In these or similar words, the priest invites the penitent to have trust in God.*

May God, who has enlightened every heart,
help you to know your sins
and trust in his mercy.
R. Amen.

*Then the priest reads from the Scripture a text that proclaims God's mercy and calls us to repentance. The penitent then makes a confession of sins. The priest gives suitable counsel and proposes an act of penance.*

*The penitent then expresses sorrow through one of the following prayers or in similar words:*

A  My God,
I am sorry for my sins with all my heart.
In choosing to do wrong
and failing to do good,
I have sinned against you
whom I should love above all things.
I firmly intend, with your help,
to do penance,
to sin no more,
and to avoid whatever leads me to sin.
Our Savior Jesus Christ
suffered and died for us.
In his name, my God, have mercy.

B  Lord Jesus, Son of God,
have mercy on me, a sinner.

C  Lord Jesus,
   you chose to be called the friend of sinners.
   By your saving death and resurrection
   free me from my sins.
   May your peace take root in my heart
   and bring forth a harvest
   of love, holiness, and truth.

   *The priest extends his hands over the penitent and speaks the words of absolution. In conclusion, the priest may say:*

Give thanks to the Lord, for he is good.

   *The penitent responds:*

His mercy endures for ever.

   *Then the priest dismisses the penitent with these or similar words:*

The Lord has freed you from your sins. Go in peace.

# PRAYERS DURING SICKNESS

## BLESSING OF THE SICK

In times of serious illness, a priest, deacon, or a lay minister will come to visit and bless the sick, and to bring holy communion. A family should advise the parish priest when a family member is seriously ill or injured so that the person may be anointed. It is fitting that the sick be blessed, perhaps daily, by other members of the household. Sometimes, this may be simply the prayer of blessing or the short form of blessing that concludes the following rite. At other times, the inclusion of a suitable scripture reading and time for prayers of intercession will be appropriate. Prayers for a sick child are on page 232.

*All make the sign of the cross. The leader begins:*

Let us bless the Lord,
who went about doing good and healing the sick.
Blessed be God now and for ever.

*All respond:*

Blessed be God for ever.

*Then the Scripture is read. A reading should be selected from the Bible, perhaps one of the Scriptures from the past Sunday's liturgy. If the illness is over a long period, the readings could be selected each day so that one of the gospels is read continuously. The following Scriptures are appropriate but should not limit the choice of a reading.*

A   Listen to the words of the apostle Paul to the Romans:

I urge you, therefore, brothers [and sisters], by the mercies of God, to offer your bodies as a living sacrifice, holy and pleasing to God, your spiritual worship. Do not conform yourself to this age but be transformed by the renewal of your mind, that you may discern what is the will of God, what is good and pleasing and perfect.

Romans 12:1-2

Or:

**B** Listen to the words of the holy gospel according to Matthew:

Moving on from [Tyre and Sidon,] Jesus walked by the Sea of Galilee, went up on the mountain, and sat down there. Great crowds came to him, having with them the lame, the blind, the deformed, the mute, and many others. They placed them at his feet, and he cured them. The crowds were amazed when they saw the mute speaking, the deformed made whole, the lame walking, and the blind able to see, and they glorified the God of Israel.

Matthew 15:29-31

*The reader concludes:*

This is the Gospel of the Lord.

*All respond:*

Praise to you, Lord Jesus Christ.

*There is a time of silence after the Scripture, then all join in prayers of intercession and in the Lord's Prayer. The leader and other members may wish to make the sign of the cross on the forehead of the one who is sick or simply place a hand on the person during the prayer.*

**A** Lord, our God,
who watches over your creatures with
unfailing care,
keep us in the safe embrace of your love.

With your strong right hand raise up your
    servant, N.,
and give him/her the strength of your own
    power.
Minister to him/her and heal his/her illness,
so that he/she may have from you the help
    he/she longs for.

We ask this through Christ our Lord.
R. Amen.

Or:

B   Lord and Father, almighty and eternal God,
    by your blessing you give us strength
        and support in our frailty:
    turn with kindness toward this your
        servant, N.
    Free him/her from all illness and restore
        him/her to health,
    so that in the sure knowledge of your
        goodness
    he/she will gratefully bless your holy name.

We ask this through Christ our Lord.
R. Amen.

*All make the sign of the cross as the leader
concludes:*

May the Lord Jesus Christ,
who went about doing good and healing the sick,
grant that we may have good health
and be enriched by his blessings.
R. Amen.

*Sometimes, a short blessing is used alone,
especially at the end of the day:*

A   May the Lord bless us,
    protect us from all evil,
    and bring us to everlasting life.
    R. Amen.

Or:

B   May the almighty and merciful God bless and
        protect us,
    the Father, and the Son, and the Holy Spirit.
    R. Amen.

## COMMUNION OF THE SICK OR ELDERLY

When a minister of the Church (who may be a member of the family) brings communion, the sick or elderly person shares in the eucharistic meal of the community. This holy communion manifests the support and concern of the community for its members who are not able to be present. The holy communion is a bond to the community as it is a union with Christ. When the eucharist is brought to the home, the family should prepare a table with a cloth and lighted candle. All members of the household may receive communion with the sick person according to the usual norms. The following texts are among many that may be chosen from the *Rite of Communion of the Sick.*

*All make the sign of the cross. The minister of communion speaks the following or a similar greeting:*

Peace be with this house and with all who live here.

*All respond:*

And also with you.

*The blessed sacrament is placed on the table. The sick person and all present may be sprinkled with holy water. Before this sprinkling, the minister of communion says:*

Let this water call to mind our baptism into Christ, who by his death and resurrection has redeemed us.

*The minister of communion then invites all to join in the penitential rite:*

My brothers and sisters, let us turn with confidence to the Lord and ask forgiveness for all our sins.

*After a brief silence, all may recite the "I confess" prayer (page 91) or the minister may speak the following invocations to which all respond.*

Lord Jesus, you healed the sick: Lord, have mercy.
R. Lord, have mercy.

Lord Jesus, you forgave sinners: Christ, have mercy.
R. Christ, have mercy.

Lord Jesus, you give us yourself to heal us
and to bring us strength: Lord, have mercy.
R. Lord have mercy.

*Then the minister concludes the penitential rite:*

May almighty God have mercy on us,
forgive us our sins,
and bring us to everlasting life.
R. Amen.

*Then the Scripture is read. An appropriate
reading should be selected and prepared by the
family or the minster of communion. The
following Scriptures are appropriate but should
not limit the choice of a reading.*

A   Listen to the words of the holy gospel
according to John:

I am the vine, you are the branches. Whoever
remains in me and I in him will bear much fruit,
because without me you can do nothing.

John 15:5

*The reader concludes:*

This is the Gospel of the Lord.

*All respond:*

Praise to you, Lord Jesus Christ.

Or:

**B** Listen to the words of the first letter of John:

We have come to know and to believe in the love
    God has for us.
God is love, and whoever remains in love
    remains in God and God in him.

1 John 4:16

*The reader concludes:*

This is the Word of the Lord.

*All respond:*

Thanks be to God.

> *Following a time of silence, all join in prayers of*
> *intercession. Then, in preparation for holy*
> *communion, all recite the Lord's Prayer. After*
> *this, the minister shows the eucharistic bread to*
> *those present, saying:*

**A** This is the bread of life.
    Taste and see that the Lord is good.

Or:

**B** This is the Lamb of God
    who takes away the sins of the world.
    Happy are those who are called to his supper.

*All who are to receive communion respond:*

Lord, I am not worthy to receive you,
but only say the word and I shall be healed.

> *The minister gives communion saying, "The Body
> of Christ," "The Blood of Christ," as appropriate.
> The sick person answers "Amen." All who wish
> receive communion in the usual way.*

> *After a time of silence, the minister says the
> following or another prayer:*

All-powerful and everliving God,
may the Body and Blood of Christ your Son
be for our brother/sister N.
a lasting remedy for body and soul.

We ask this through Christ our Lord.
R. Amen.

> *The rite concludes with a blessing:*

A   May the Lord bless us,
protect us from all evil,
and bring us to everlasting life.
R. Amen.

Or:

B   May the almighty and merciful God bless and
protect us,
the Father, and the Son, and the Holy Spirit.
R. Amen.

# ANOINTING OF THE SICK

The following notes, taken from the Church's book *Pastoral Care of the Sick* (nos. 5-6, 8-15, 99-100), will be helpful in understanding the sacrament of anointing and in knowing when the parish priest should be asked to celebrate this sacrament with the family and the sick person.

"The Lord himself showed great concern for the bodily and spiritual welfare of the sick and commanded his followers to do likewise. This is clear from the gospels, and above all from the existence of the sacrament of anointing, which he instituted and which is made known in the Letter of James. Since then the Church has never ceased to celebrate this sacrament for its members by the anointing and the prayer of its priests, commending those who are ill to the suffering and glorified Lord, that he may raise them up and save them (see James 5:14-16). Moreover, the Church exhorts them to associate themselves willingly with the passion and death of Christ (see Romans 8:17), and thus contribute to the welfare of the people of God.

"Those who are seriously ill need the special help of God's grace in this time of anxiety, lest they be broken in spirit and, under the pressure of temptation, perhaps weakened in their faith.

"This is why, through the sacrament of anointing, Christ strengthens the faithful who are afflicted by illness, providing them with the strongest means of support.

"The celebration of this sacrament consists especially in the laying on of hands by the priests of the Church, the offering of the prayer of faith, and the anointing of the sick with oil made holy by God's blessing. This rite signifies the grace of the sacrament and confers it.

"This sacrament gives the grace of the Holy Spirit to those who are sick: by this grace the whole person is helped and saved, sustained by trust in God, and strengthened against the temptations of the Evil One and against anxiety over death. Thus the sick person is able not only to bear suffering bravely, but also to fight against it. A return to physical health may follow the reception of this sacrament if it will be beneficial to the sick person's salvation. If necessary, the sacrament also provides the sick person with the forgiveness of sins and the completion of Christian penance. . . .

"The Letter of James states that the sick are to be anointed in order to raise them up and save them. Great care and concern should be taken to see that those of the faithful whose health is seriously impaired by sickness or old age receive this sacrament.

"A prudent or reasonably sure judgment, without scruple, is sufficient for deciding on the seriousness of an illness; if necessary a doctor may be consulted.

"The sacrament may be repeated if the sick person recovers after being anointed and then again falls ill or if during the same illness the person's condition becomes more serious.

"A sick person may be anointed before surgery whenever a serious illness is the reason for the surgery.

"Elderly people may be anointed if they have become notably weakened even though no serious illness is present.

"Sick children may be anointed if they have sufficient use of reason to be strengthened by this sacrament. . . .

"When a priest has been called to attend those who are already dead, he should not administer the sacrament of anointing. Instead, he should pray for them, asking that God forgive their sins and graciously receive them into the kingdom. . . .

"Because of its very nature as a sign, the sacrament of the anointing of the sick should be celebrated with members of the family and other representatives of the Christian community whenever this is possible. Then the sacrament is seen for what it is—a part of the prayer of the Church and an encounter with the Lord. The sign of the sacrament will be further enhanced by avoiding undue haste in prayer and action.

"The priest should inquire about the physical and spiritual condition of the sick person and he should become acquainted with the family, friends, and others who may be present. The sick person and others may help to plan the celebration, for example, by choosing the readings and prayers. It will be especially helpful if the sick person, the priest, and the family become accustomed to praying together.

"In the choice of readings the condition of the sick person should be kept in mind. The readings and the homily should help those present to reach a deeper understanding of the mystery of human suffering in relation to the paschal mystery of Christ."

*The anointing of the sick begins much as the communion of the sick on page 256. After the reading of Scripture (and homily), the following litany is prayed. All respond "Lord, have mercy" to each petition.*

*The minister says:*

My brother and sisters, in our prayer of faith let
us appeal to God for our brother/sister N.

Come and strengthen him/her through this holy
   anointing: Lord, have mercy. R.
Free him/her from all harm: Lord, have mercy. R.
Free him/her from sin and all temptations: Lord,
   have mercy. R.
Relieve the sufferings of all the sick: Lord, have
   mercy. R.
Assist all those dedicated to the care of the sick:
   Lord, have mercy. R.
Give life and health to our brother/sister N., on
   whom we lay our hands in your name: Lord,
   have mercy. R.

*After the laying on of hands, the priest gives
thanks over the oil of the sick, then anoints the
forehead and hands of the sick person. He may
also anoint other parts of the body, for example,
the area of pain or injury. A prayer follows the
anointing, then all join in the Lord's Prayer. If
the sick person is to receive communion, others
present may also receive. The anointing concludes
with the blessing of the sick person and of all
present.*

# PRAYERS OF THE SICK

Those who are sick should make use of many of the prayers throughout this book, and especially those in Part V. Sometimes, short prayers, repeated slowly over and over, are most appropriate.


Lord Jesus Christ,
Son of the living God,
have mercy on me.


Praised be Jesus Christ.


Lord, I hope in you.


Your will be done.


Strengthen me, Lord.


Lord, have mercy.


Sacred Heart of Jesus, have mercy on us.


My Lord and my God.


Jesus, Mary, and Joseph.

Pray for us, holy Mother of God,
that we may become worthy of the promises of
Christ.


Holy Mary, pray for us.

# PRAYERS AT THE TIME OF DEATH

As death approaches, the Church stays close to the one who is dying, to give comfort and support. The family should ask that holy communion be brought to the dying. This is viaticum, "food for the journey." Members of the local Church may wish to join the family in a vigil of prayer. After death, the family is encouraged to continue in prayer, to take part in the preparation of the vigil (wake) and funeral liturgies, and to participate in the preparation of the body for burial. In all of these moments, many of the traditional prayers of the Church may be chosen (see Part V).

The prayers below are from the many beautiful texts with which the Church commends the dying to God and celebrates the funeral and burial rites.

The Church's book of prayers for the sick and the dying, *Pastoral Care of the Sick* (no. 213), speaks of the response of the Christian Church to its dying members in these words:

> Christians have the responsibility of expressing their union in Christ by joining the dying person in prayer for God's mercy and for confidence in Christ. In particular, the presence of a priest or deacon shows more clearly that the Christian dies in the communion of the Church. He should assist the dying person and those present in the recitation of the prayers of commendation and, following death, he should lead those present in the prayer after death. If the priest or deacon is unable to be present because of other serious pastoral obligations, other members of the community should be prepared to assist with these prayers and should have the texts readily available to them.

## VIATICUM

Viaticum is the sacrament of the dying. When the minister has brought holy communion, the rite may begin with the renewal of the dying person's profession of faith (page 371). Viaticum is then celebrated in the same manner as communion of the sick (page 256), but after giving communion, the minister says:

May the Lord Jesus Christ protect you
and lead you to eternal life.
R. Amen.

*The concluding prayer follows:*

God of peace,
you offer eternal healing to those who believe in
    you;
you have refreshed your servant N.
with food and drink from heaven:
lead him/her safely into the kingdom of light.

We ask this through Christ our Lord.
R. Amen.

# PRAYERS WITH THE DYING

The following are some of the prayers that may be
recited with the dying person, alternating with times
of silence. Sometimes, the same prayer should be
repeated many times (see the prayers on page 270).
When the dying person cannot take part, those who
are present continue to pray. In such prayers, the
paschal character of a Christian's death is made
manifest. The Our Father, Hail Mary, Glory Be, and
many of the prayers in Part V are also appropriate.
The dying person may be signed on the forehead
with the cross, as was done at baptism.

## SHORT TEXTS

What will separate us from the love of Christ?

Romans 8:35

Whether we live or die, we are the Lord's.

Romans 14:8

We shall always be with the Lord.

1 Thessalonians 4:17

To you I lift up my soul, O LORD.

Psalm 25:1

Even though I walk in the dark valley,
I fear no evil; for you are at my side.

Psalm 23:4

Into your hands, LORD, I commend my spirit.

Psalm 31:5a

Jesus, remember me when you come into your kingdom.

Luke 23:42

Lord Jesus, receive my spirit.

Acts 7:59

Holy Mary, pray for me.

Saint Joseph, pray for me.

Jesus, Mary, and Joseph,
assist me in my last agony.

## SCRIPTURE READINGS

Among many appropriate scripture readings are the
following: Job 19:23-27; Psalm 23; Psalm 25; Psalm
91; Psalm 121; 1 John 4:16; Revelation 21:1-7; Matthew 25:1-13; Luke 22:39-46; Luke 23:44-49; Luke
24:1-8; John 6:37-40; John 14:1 6,23,27.

## PRAYERS OF COMMENDATION

*As the time of death approaches, this prayer may
be said.*

Go forth, Christian soul, from this world
in the name of God the almighty Father,
who created you,
in the name of Jesus Christ, Son of the
    living God,
who suffered for you,
in the name of the Holy Spirit,
who was poured out upon you,
go forth, faithful Christian.

May you live in peace this day,
may your home be with God in Zion,
with Mary, the virgin Mother of God,
with Joseph, and all the angels and saints.

## PRAYERS AFTER DEATH

The following prayers may be recited immediately
after death and may be repeated in the hours that
follow.


Saints of God, come to his/her aid!
Come to meet him/her, angels of the Lord!
R. Receive his/her soul and present him/her
to God the Most High.

May Christ, who called you, take you to himself;
may angels lead you to Abraham's side. R.

Give him/her eternal rest, O Lord,
and may your light shine on him/her for ever. R.

Let us pray.

All-powerful and merciful God,
we commend to you N., your servant.
In your mercy and love,
blot out the sins he/she has committed
    through human weakness.
In this world he/she has died:
let him/her live with you for ever.

We ask this through Christ our Lord.
R. Amen.

*These verses may also be used.*

V. Eternal rest grant unto him/her, O Lord.
R. And let perpetual light shine upon him/her.

V. May he/she rest in peace.
R. Amen.

V. May his/her soul and the souls of all the faithful departed, through the mercy of God, rest in peace.
R. Amen.

# GATHERING IN THE PRESENCE OF THE BODY

When the family first gathers around the body, before or after it is prepared for burial, all or some of the following prayers may be used. It is most fitting that family members take part in preparing the body for burial.

*All make the sign of the cross:*

In the name of the Father, and of the Son, and of the Holy Spirit.
R. Amen.

*Then one member of the family reads:*

My brothers and sisters, Jesus says: "Come to me, all you who labor and are overburdened, and I will give you rest. Shoulder my yoke and learn from me, for I am gentle and humble in heart, and you will find rest for your souls. Yes, my yoke is easy and my burden light."

*The body may then be sprinkled with holy water:*

The Lord God lives in his holy temple
   yet abides in our midst.
Since in baptism N. became God's temple
and the Spirit of God lived in him/her,
with reverence we bless his/her mortal body.

*Then one member of the family may say:*

With God there is mercy and fullness of redemption; let us pray as Jesus taught us: Our Father. . . .

*Then this prayer is said:*

Into your hands, O Lord,
we humbly entrust our brother/sister N.
In this life you embraced him/her with your
   tender love;
deliver him/her now from every evil
and bid him/her enter eternal rest.

The old order has passed away:
welcome him/her then into paradise,
where there will be no sorrow, no weeping nor
    pain,
but the fullness of peace and joy
with your Son and the Holy Spirit
for ever and ever.
R. Amen.

> *All may sign the forehead of the deceased with the
> sign of the cross. One member of the family says:*

Blessed are those who have died in the Lord;
let them rest from their labors
for their good deeds go with them.

V. Eternal rest grant unto him/her, O Lord.
R. And let perpetual light shine upon him/her.

V. May he/she rest in peace.
R. Amen.

V. May his/her soul and the souls of all the
    faithful departed, through the mercy of God,
    rest in peace.
R. Amen.

> *All make the sign of the cross as one member of
> the family says:*

May the love of God and the peace of the Lord
   Jesus Christ
bless and console us
and gently wipe every tear from our eyes:
in the name of the Father,
and of the Son, and of the Holy Spirit.
R. Amen.


## PRAYERS FOR MOURNERS

The final prayer from the previous section ("May
the love of God") or one of the following prayers
may be used by those in mourning.


Lord God,
you are attentive to the voice of our pleading.
Let us find in your Son
comfort in our sadness,
certainty in our doubt,
and courage to live through this hour.
Make our faith strong
through Christ our Lord.
R. Amen.


Lord,
N. is gone now from this earthly dwelling,
and has left behind those who mourn his/her
   absence.
Grant that we may hold his/her memory dear,
never bitter for what we have lost
nor in regret for the past,
but always in hope of the eternal kingdom
where you will bring us together again.

We ask this through Christ our Lord.
R. Amen.

*For those who mourn the death of a child:*

O Lord, whose ways are beyond understanding,
listen to the prayers of your faithful people:
that those weighed down by grief
at the loss of this (little) child
may we find reassurance in your infinite
goodness.

We ask this through Christ our Lord.
R. Amen.

# BLESSING OF PARENTS AFTER A MISCARRIAGE

When a baby dies before birth, the parents may
seek the prayers of the Church. A priest, deacon,
lay minister of the parish, or a member of the family
may lead this blessing.

*All make the sign of the cross. The leader begins:*

Let us praise the Father of mercies, the God of all
consolation. Blessed be God for ever.

*All respond:*

Blessed be God for ever.

*The leader may use these or similar words to
introduce the blessing:*

For those who trust in God,
in the pain of sorrow there is consolation,
in the face of despair there is hope,
in the midst of death there is life.

N. and N., as we mourn the death of your child,
we place ourselves in the hands of God and ask
strength, for healing and for love.

*Then the Scripture is read:*

Listen to the words of the book of Lamentations:

My soul is deprived of peace,
   I have forgotten what happiness is;
I tell myself my future is lost,
   all that I hoped for from the LORD.

But I will call this to mind,
   as my reason to have hope:
The favors of the LORD are not exhausted,
   his mercies are not spent;
They are renewed each morning,
   so great is his faithfulness.
My portion is the LORD, says my soul;
   therefore I will hope in him.

Lamentations 3:17-18,21-24

*The reader concludes:*

This is the Word of the Lord.

*All respond:*

Thanks be to God.

*After a time of silence, all join in prayers of intercession. These conclude with the Lord's Prayer. Then the leader may invite all to extend their hands over the parents in blessing.*

Father and Creator,
in whom all life and death find meaning,
we bless you at all times,
especially when we have need of your
   consolation.

N. and N. entrust to your care a life conceived in
   love.
May your blessing come upon them now.
Remove all anxiety from their minds
and strengthen this love
so that they may have peace in their hearts and
   home.

We ask this through Christ our Lord.
R. Amen.

*All make the sign of the cross as the leader concludes:*

May the almighty and merciful God bless and
   protect us,
the Father, the Son, and the Holy Spirit.
R. Amen.

# PRAYERS AT THE GRAVESIDE

During the time of mourning, the following prayers my be recited at the graveside. The prayers given on page 178 are appropriate whenever visiting a grave.

A   Lord Jesus Christ,
    by your own three days in the tomb,
    you hallowed the graves of all who believe in
      you
    and so made the grave a sign of hope
    that promises resurrection
    even as it claims our mortal bodies.

    Grant that our brother/sister, N., may sleep
      here in peace
    until you awaken him/her to glory,
    for you are the resurrection and the life.
    Then he/she will see you face to face
    and in your light will see light
    and know the splendor of God,
    for you live and reign for ever and ever.
    R. Amen.

B   O God,
    by whose mercy the faithful departed find
      rest,
    send your holy angel to watch over this
      grave.

    We ask this through Christ our Lord.
    R. Amen.

# PART IV
# BLESSINGS FOR
# VARIOUS
# TIMES AND PLACES

# INTRODUCTION

These blessings of persons are meant for various occasions and events in the course of life. These are moments for thanksgiving and intercession. The changes in our lives and families, the work we do, the wrong we do, the times of joy—all are brought before God in prayer. The forms of these blessing vary from short prayers to more structured rites. Many times, these texts will be best used within the table blessing.

## PRAYER FOR WELCOMING GUESTS

When the household welcomes guests, this psalm may be prayed at table or another time.

The LORD is my shepherd; I shall not want.
    In verdant pastures he gives me repose;
Beside restful waters he leads me;
    he refreshes my soul.
He guides me in right paths
    for his name's sake.
Even though I walk in the dark valley
    I fear no evil; for you are at my side
With your rod and your staff
    that give me courage.

You spread a table before me
  in the sight of my foes;
You anoint my head with oil;
  my cup overflows.
Only goodness and kindness follow me
  all the days of my life;
And I shall dwell in the house of the LORD
  for years to come.

Psalm 23

*To the guests:*

May grace be yours
and peace in abundance from God,
now and for ever.
R. Amen.


## PRAYER WHEN GATHERING TO MEET OR STUDY

When the household is host to a meeting, various prayers may be chosen, as appropriate, from those given in Part I for evening or nighttime. There may be a place for reading the Scripture and for prayers of intercession. On occasion, the invocation of the Holy Spirit (page 157) may be a fitting prayer.

*If the purpose of the meeting is the study of Scripture, the following prayer is appropriate:*

Lord our God,
we bless you.
As we come together to ponder the Scriptures,
we ask you in your kindness
to fill us with the knowledge of your will
so that, pleasing you in all things,
we may grow in every good work.

We ask this through Christ our Lord.
R. Amen.

*Any meeting may conclude with this blessing:*

May God, the source of all patience and
    encouragement,
enable us to live in perfect harmony with one
    another
in the spirit of Christ Jesus.
With one heart and one voice
may we glorify God,
now and for ever.
R. Amen.

*The Lord's Prayer may follow.*

## BLESSING BEFORE LEAVING ON A JOURNEY

When one or several members of the household are
to be absent from the household for some length
of time, they may be blessed just before their departure. If an entire family is preparing to travel, the
words of the blessing are altered as necessary. The
words of the final blessing alone may be used for
those who travel often.

*All make the sign of the cross. The leader begins:*

May the Lord turn his face toward us and guide
our feet into the way of peace, now and for ever.

*All respond:*

Blessed be God for ever.

*The leader may use these or similar words to
introduce the blessing:*

Let us entrust those who are leaving to the hands
of the Lord. Let us pray that he will give them a
prosperous journey and that as they travel, they
will praise him in all his creatures; that they will
experience God's own goodness in the hospitality
they receive and bring the Good News of
salvation to all those they meet; that they will be
courteous toward all; that they will greet the poor
and afflicted with kindness and know how to
comfort and help them.

*Then the Scripture is read:*

Listen to the words of the book of Tobit:

[Tobit] called his son and said to him: "My son,
prepare whatever you need for the journey, and
set out with your kinsman. May God in heaven
protect you on the way and bring you back to me
safe and sound; and may his angel accompany
you for safety, my son."

Before setting out on his journey, Tobiah kissed his father and mother. Tobit said to him, "Have a safe journey." But his mother began to weep.

Tobit reassured her: ". . . Our son will leave in good health and come back to us in good health. Your own eyes will see the day when he returns to you safe and sound. So, no such thought; do not worry about them, my love. For a good angel will go with him, his journey will be successful, and he will return unharmed."

Tobit 5:17b-18a,21-22

*(The family's Bible may be used for an alternate reading such as Genesis 28:10-16 or Deuteronomy 6:4-9.)*

*The reader concludes:*

This is the Word of the Lord.

*All respond:*

Thanks be to God.

*After a time of silence, all join in prayers of intercession and in the Lord's Prayer. Those remaining at home may place their hands on the heads of those who are making the journey while the prayer A is used. If all are making the journey, the prayer B is used.*

A All-powerful and merciful God,
   you led the children of Israel on dry land,
      parting the waters of the sea;
   you guided the Magi to your Son by a star.

Help our brother/sister, N.,
(OR: Help these our brothers and sisters, N.
   and N.)
   and give him/her (them) a safe journey.
Under your protection let him/her (them)
   reach their destination
and come at last to the eternal haven of
   salvation.

We ask this through Christ our Lord.
R. Amen.

Or:

**B**   All-powerful and ever-living God,
   when Abraham left his own land
   and departed from his own people,
   you kept him safe all through his journey.
   Protect us, who also are your servants:
   walk by our side to help us;
   be our companion and our strength on the
      road
   and our refuge in every adversity.
   Lead us, O Lord,
   so that we will reach our destination in safety
   and happily return to our home(s).

We ask this through Christ our Lord.
R. Amen.

*All make the sign of the cross as the leader
concludes:*

A   May God bless you with every heavenly
        blessing
    and give you a safe journey;
    wherever life leads you,
    may you find him there to protect you.

    We ask this through Christ our Lord.
        Amen.

Or:

B   May almighty God bless us
    and hear our prayers for a safe journey.
        Amen.

Or:

C   In paths of peace may the Lord God guide
        you/us,
    and may he send his holy angel Raphael
    to accompany you/us on your/our way:
    that safe and sound, in peace and in joy,
    you/we may return to those who love you/us.

    We ask this through Christ our Lord.
    R. Amen.

*The blessing may conclude with song. The
following is appropriate and may be sung to a
tune such as "The Old Hundreth" (Praise God
from Whom All Blessings Flow).*

I sing as I arise today!
I call on my Creator's might;
The will of God to be my guide,
The eye of God to be my sight.

The word of God to be my speech,
The hand of God to be my stay,
The shield of God to be my strength,
The path of God to be my way.

## BLESSING UPON RETURNING FROM A JOURNEY

When one or several members of the household have been away for some time, they may be blessed upon their return. The blessing may take place at table or at another time. If all the members of the household have been gone, the words are changed accordingly.

*All make the sign of the cross. The leader begins:*

Peace be with this house and with all who live here. Blessed be the name of the Lord.

*All respond:*

Now and for ever.

*The leader may use these or similar words to introduce the blessing:*

Join now in praising God for a journey safely ended and for the home we share, for all that we have seen of God's goodness and for all those we met on our way. Remember that God commands us to welcome the homeless and to shelter the stranger.

*Then the Scripture is read:*

Listen to the words of the holy gospel according to Matthew:

[Jesus said:] "Come to me, all you who labor and are burdened, and I will give you rest. Take my yoke upon you and learn from me, for I am meek and humble of heart; and you will find rest for yourselves. For my yoke is easy, and my burden light."

Matthew 11:28-30

*The reader concludes:*

This is the Gospel of the Lord.

*All respond:*

Praise to you, Lord Jesus Christ

*After a time of silence, all may join in prayers of thanksgiving and intercession and in the Lord's Prayer. The leader then speaks the prayer of blessing:*

Blessed are you, Lord our God,
for you lead us by separate ways,
and you return us to one another.
In loving kindness you have given us a place to
    be at home.
Keep us in your care through all our pilgrimage
until we find our home with you.

We ask this through Christ our Lord.
R. Amen.

Let us bless the Lord.

Thanks be to God.

*The blessing may conclude with song:*

Now thank we all our God with hearts and
  hands and voices,
Who wondrous things has done, in whom this
  world rejoices;
Who, from our mothers' arms, has blessed us on
  our way
With countless gifts of love, and still in ours
  today.

O may this gracious God through all our life be
  near us,
With ever joyful hearts and blessed peace to
  cheer us;
Preserve us in this grace, and guide us in
  distress,
And free us from all sin, till heaven we possess.

Martin Rinkart

# BLESSING BEFORE LEAVING HOME FOR SCHOOL, EMPLOYMENT, OR MINISTRY

When a member of the household prepares to move away or leave for a prolonged time, this blessing may be part of the prayer at table or at some other time.

*All make the sign of the cross. The leader begins:*

The Lord will guard your coming and your going. Blessed be the name of the Lord.

*All respond:*

Now and for ever.

*The leader may use these or similar words to introduce the blessing:*

Gathering all our memories of good times and difficulties together, and full of hope and concern for the days ahead, let us ask God's blessing on N.

*Then the Scripture is read:*

Listen to the words of the holy gospel according to John:

Thomas said to [Jesus], "Master, we do not know where you are going; how can we know the way?" Jesus said to him, "I am the way and the truth and the life. No one comes to the Father except through me."

John 14:5-6

*(The family's Bible may be used for an alternate reading such as Genesis 12:1-9.)*

*The reader concludes:*

This is the Gospel of the Lord.

*All respond:*

Praise to you, Lord Jesus Christ.

*All join in prayers of intercession and in the Lord's Prayer. A Bible may be given by the family to the one who is leaving. Then all may extend their hands toward the one who is leaving as the leader speaks the blessing:*

A   O God, you led your servant Abraham from
      his home
   and guarded him in all his wanderings.
   Guide this servant of yours, N.
   Be a refuge on the journey, shade in the heat,
   shelter in the storm, rest in weariness,
   protection in trouble, and a strong staff in
      danger.
   For all our days together, we give you
      thanks:
   bind us together now, even though we may
      be far apart.

May your peace rest upon this house,
and may it go with your servant always.

Grant this through Christ our Lord.
R. Amen.

Or:

*The following prayer is appropriate for one leaving
to work in Christian ministry:*

B   God our Father,
    you will all men to be saved
    and come to the knowledge of the truth.
    Send workers into your great harvest
    that the Gospel may be preached to every
        creature
    and your people, gathered together by the
        word of life
    and strengthened by the power of the
        sacraments,
    may advance in the way of salvation and
        love.

Grant this through Christ our Lord.
R. Amen.

*A sign of God's peace may be extended to the one
who is leaving.*

*The leader says:*

Let us bless the Lord.

*All respond, making the sign of the cross:*

Thanks be to God.

*The blessing may conclude with a song such as "Now Thank We All Our God" (page 291) or "I Sing as I Arise Today" (page 288).*

# BLESSING BEFORE MOVING FROM A HOME

When a family is about to leave a house or apartment where they have lived, they may wish to mark the departure with thanksgiving and intercession. The blessing may begin by walking together through the rooms and speaking of the life lived in each. Then all gather before a cross or icon that is still in place.

*All make the sign of the cross. The leader begins:*

Blessed be the Lord,
a merciful and gracious God,
rich in kindness and fidelity.
Blessed be God for ever.

*All respond:*

Blessed be God for ever.

*The leader may use these or similar words to introduce the blessing:*

As we leave this home, we give thanks to God for all the blessings found here. We ask forgiveness for the wrong we have done one another. Let us pray now that God will guide us on our way.

*Psalm 23 (page 282) or Psalm 121 (page 242) may be read by one or by all together. Then all may join in prayers of thanksgiving and intercession and in the Lord's Prayer. The leader then speaks the prayer of blessing.*

God, our refuge,
our home is ever with you.
May these rooms where we have lived
and found both joys and sorrows
be a place of blessing for those
   who will live here after us.
Protect us on our way;
lead us to new friends;
help us to be a home to one another
and to all who need the love and shelter that is
   ours,
till at last we come to our eternal home with you.

Grant this through Christ our Lord.
R. Amen.

*The cross or icon is taken from its place and all reverence it with a kiss.*

*The leader says:*

Let us bless the Lord.

*All respond, making the sign of the cross:*

Thanks be to God.

*The blessing may conclude with a song (for example, "Now Thank We All Our God" page 291).*

# BLESSING UPON MOVING INTO A NEW HOME

Guests may be invited for the blessing of an individual's or family's home. All gather where the cross or icon will be placed.

*All make the sign of the cross. The leader begins:*

Peace be with this house and with all who live here. Blessed be the name of the Lord.

*All respond:*

Now and for ever.

*The leader may use these or similar words to introduce the blessing:*

When Christ took flesh through the Blessed Virgin Mary, he made his home with us. Let us now pray that he will enter this home and bless it with his presence. May he always be here among us; may he nurture our love for each other, share in our joys, comfort us in our sorrows. Inspired by his teachings and example, let us seek to make our new home before all else a dwelling place of love, diffusing far and wide the goodness of Christ.

*Then the Scripture is read:*

Listen to the words of the holy gospel according to Luke:

As they continued their journey [Jesus] entered a village where a woman whose name was Martha welcomed him. She had a sister named Mary [who] sat beside the Lord at his feet listening to him speak. Martha, burdened with much serving, came to him and said, "Lord, do you not care that my sister has left me by myself to do the serving? Tell her to help me." The Lord said to her in reply, "Martha, Martha, you are anxious and worried about many things. There is need of only one thing. Mary has chosen the better part and it will not be taken from her."

Luke 10:38-42

*(The family's Bible may be used for an alternate reading such as Luke 10:5-9; Genesis 18:1-10; or Luke 19:1-9.)*

*The reader concludes:*

This is the Gospel of the Lord.

*All respond:*

Praise to you, Lord Jesus Christ.

*All go from room to room, offering prayers of
intercession and sprinkling holy water, if desired.
Some of the following prayers may be used.*

*At the entrance:*

O God, protect our going out and our coming in;
let us share the hospitality of this home
    with all who visit us,
that those who enter here may know your love
    and peace.

Grant this through Christ our Lord.
R. Amen.

*In the living room:*

O God, give your blessing to all who share this
    room,
that we may be knit together in companionship.

Grant this through Christ our Lord.
R. Amen.

*In the kitchen:*

O God, you fill the hungry with good things.
Send your blessing on us, as we work in this
    kitchen,
and make us ever thankful for our daily bread.

Grant this through Christ our Lord.
R. Amen.

*In the dining room:*

Blessed are you, Lord of heaven and earth,
for you give us food and drink to sustain our
   lives
and make our hearts glad.
Help us grateful for all your mercies,
and mindful of the needs of others.

Grant this through Christ our Lord.
R. Amen.

*In the bedroom(s):*

Protect us, Lord, as we stay awake;
watch over us us as we sleep,
that awake we may keep watch with Christ,
and asleep, we may rest in his peace.

Grant this through Christ our Lord.
R. Amen.

*In the bathroom:*

Blessed are you, Lord of heaven and earth.
You formed us in wisdom and love.
Refresh us in body and in spirit,
and keep us in good health that we might serve
you.

Grant this through Christ our Lord.
R. Amen.

*All return to the starting place. A cross or icon is kissed by each person, then put in a permanent place of honor. A candle may be lighted before it. Then all recite the Lord's Prayer. The leader speaks the prayer of blessing:*

Be our shelter, Lord, when we are at home,
our companion when we are away,
and our welcome guest when we return.
And at last receive us into the dwelling place
  you have prepared for us
in your Father's house,
where you live for ever and ever.
R. Amen.

*All make the sign of the cross as the leader concludes:*

May the peace of Christ rule in our hearts,
and may the word of Christ in all its richness
  dwell in us,
so that whatever we do in word and in work,
we will do in the name of the Lord.
R. Amen.

*The blessing may conclude with a song such as "Now Thank We All Our God," page 291.*

## BLESSING FOR A PLACE OF WORK

When a place of work is blessed, both those who labor there and those who share the fruit of that labor should be invited.

*All make the sign of the cross. The leader begins:*

Blessed be God,
who has begun a good work in us.
Blessed be the name of the Lord.

*All respond:*

Now and for ever.

*The leader may use these or similar words to introduce the blessing:*

Jesus showed us the dignity of labor. He was known as the carpenter's son, and he willingly worked with the tools of his trade. Through the labor of our hands, we bring God's blessing upon ourselves and others. Let us pray for all who will work here and for those who will share the fruit of their labor.

*Then the Scripture is read:*

Listen to the words of the apostle Paul to the Thessalonians:

We urge you, brothers [and sisters], to progress even more, and to aspire to live a tranquil life, to mind your own affairs, and to work with your [own] hands, as we instructed you, that you may conduct yourselves properly toward outsiders and not depend on anyone.

1 Thessalonians 4:10-12

*(The family's Bible may be used for an alternate reading such as Matthew 6:25-34.)*

*The reader concludes:*

This is the Word of the Lord.

*All respond:*

Thanks be to God.

> *After a time of silence, all join in prayers of intercession and in the Lord's Prayer. A cross or other symbol may then be reverenced with a kiss and put in a place of honor. The leader then speaks the prayer of blessing; one of the following may be used or adapted as needed.*

## OF AN OFFICE

O God,
in your wise providence
you are glad to bless all human labor,
the work of our hands and of our minds.
Grant that all who plan and conduct business in
   this office
may through your guidance and support
come to right decisions and carry them out fairly.

We ask this through Christ our Lord.
R. Amen.

## OF A SHOP OR FACTORY

God, our all-provident Father,
you have placed the earth and its fruits under
our care,
so that by our labor we will endeavor
to ensure that all share in the benefits of your
creation.
Bless all those who will use this building
either as buyers or sellers,
so that by respecting justice and charity
they will see themselves as working for the
common good
and find joy in contributing to the progress
of the earthly city.

We ask this through Christ our Lord.
R. Amen.

*Then holy water may be sprinkled on the place
and the participants.*

*All make the sign of the cross as the leader
concludes:*

May God, the Father of goodness,
who commanded us to help one another
as brothers and sisters,
bless this building with his presence
and look kindly on all who enter here.
R. Amen.

*The blessing may conclude with a song such as
"Now Thank We All Our God," page 291.*

# BLESSING OF OBJECTS

Sometimes, tools or objects provide an occasion to give thanks and ask God's blessing. In these prayers, we recognize the joy and responsibility of human labor, recreation, and devotion.

*For each kind of object named below, an appropriate Scripture is suggested and a short prayer of blessing. The blessing begins with the sign of the cross and the words:*

With glad hearts let us praise and bless Christ, the Son of God, who was pleased to be known as the carpenter's son. Blessed be God for ever.

*All respond:*

Blessed be God for ever.

*The leader may use these or similar words to introduce the blessing:*

Saint Paul said, "All these things are yours, and you are Christ's, and Christ is God's." To accomplish God's purpose, we use suitable objects and so in some way cooperate with him and share in the good of redemption. Let us, therefore, bless God from our hearts for his wonderful plan and pray that his help will protect and sustain us as we work.

*See below for scripture readings. After the reading, all may join in prayers of intercession and the Lord's Prayer. Then the leader says the appropriate blessing. Any of the blessings may conclude with a suitable song, such as "Now Thank We All Our God," page 291.*

## BLESSING OF TOOLS FOR WORK

Appropriate Scriptures include: Job 28:1-28; Proverbs 31:10-31; Sirach 38:24-34; Isaiah 28:23-29; Acts 18:1-5; Matthew 13:1-9; Luke 5:3-11; Timothy 4:4. Each tells of a different kind of human work.

O God,
the fullness of blessing comes down from you,
to you our prayers of blessing rise up.
In your kindness protect your servants,
who stand here before you devout and faithful,
bearing the tools of their trade.
Grant that their hard work may contribute
to the perfecting of your creation
and provide a decent life for themselves and their
    families.
Help them to strive for a better society
and to praise and glorify your holy name always.

We ask this through Christ our Lord.
R. Amen.

## BLESSING OF THE WORK OF AN ARTIST OR CRAFTSPERSON

Appropriate Scriptures include: Genesis 1;
Job 38-39; Psalm 8; Revelation 21:1-4.

God our creator,
the heavens declare your glory,
and earth proclaims your handiwork.

We praise you for the work of creation,
manifest in the imagination and skill
    of artists and craftspeople
who bring beauty and delight,
    challenge and vision to our lives.

May your blessing be upon all who share this
    work:
may we all become heralds of your reign
when beauty shall be the companion of justice
    and peace.

We ask this through Christ our Lord.
R. Amen.


## BLESSING OF OBJECTS FOR USE OR ENTERTAINMENT

Appropriate Scriptures include: Psalm 104 (selected
verses); Psalm 150 (page 355).


God,
we praise you for the work of human hands.

Bless us when these (name the objects)
 are used to renew our spirits,
to help us in our work,
or to bring us knowledge of our neighbors,
 our community and our world.
Give us wisdom and humility
to be good stewards of the earth and of our days.

We ask this through Christ our Lord.
R. Amen.


## BLESSING OF OBJECTS FOR PRAYER AND DEVOTION

This blessing may be used for icons and other
images, as well as books and candles and other
objects used within the household's prayer. Appropriate Scriptures include: Colossians 1:12-20; Luke
1:42-50; Ephesians 3:14-19; 2 Corinthians 3:17-4;
Romans 8:26-31; 1 Corinthians 13:8-13; Luke 11:5-
3; Psalm 150.


Lord,
you are blessed and the source of every blessing.
Be with us now
and whenever we use this symbol of our faith.
May we strive always to be transformed
into the likeness of Christ, your Son,
who lives and reigns for ever and ever.
R. Amen.

# BLESSING IN TIMES OF JOY AND THANKSGIVING

The Sunday eucharist is the source and model of the thanksgiving to God, which should fill the daily life of the Christian. This thanksgiving is expressed daily in morning and evening prayer and at table. Sometimes, there is reason and need for the household to give special thanks to God. The following blessing may be used. Other prayers of thanksgiving are found in Part V.

*All make the sign of the cross. The leader begins:*

Give praise to God, who is rich in mercy
and who has favored us in wonderful ways.
Blessed be God for ever.

*All respond:*

Blessed be God for ever.

*The leader may use these or similar words to introduce the blessing:*

Saint Paul urges us to give thanks to God always through Christ, for in him, God has given us everything.

*Then the Scripture is read:*

Listen to the words of the apostle Paul to the Philippians:

Rejoice in the Lord always. I shall say it again:
rejoice! Your kindness should be known to all.
The Lord is near. Have no anxiety at all, but in
everything, by prayer and petition, with
thanksgiving, make your requests known to God.
Then the peace of God that surpasses all
understanding will guard your hearts and minds
in Christ Jesus.

Philippians 4:4-7

*(The family's Bible may be used for an alternate
reading such as Colossians 3:15-17 or 1
Thessalonians 5:12-24.)*

*The reader concludes:*

This is the Word of the Lord.

*All respond:*

Thanks be to God.

*After a time of silence, all join in prayers of
intercession and in the Lord's Prayer. Then the
leader prays:*

Almighty Father,
you are lavish in bestowing all your gifts,
and we give you thanks for the favors you have
    given us.
In your goodness you have favored us
and kept us safe in the past.
We ask that you continue to protect us
and to shelter us in the shadow of your wings.

We ask this through Christ our Lord.
R. Amen.

*All make the sign of the cross as the leader
concludes:*

May God the Father, with the Son and the Holy
  Spirit,
who has shown us such great mercy,
be praised and blessed for ever and ever.
R. Amen.

*The blessing may conclude with a song such as
"Holy God, We Praise Thy Name" (page 333);
"For the Fruits of This Creation" (page 173); or
"Now Thank We All Our God" (page 291).*


# BLESSING IN TIMES OF SUFFERING AND NEED

When a member of a household is passing through
a time of anguish or great need, this blessing, or
various texts found in Part V, may be appropriate.


*All make the sign of the cross. The leader begins:*

God comforts us in all our afflictions.
Blessed be God for ever.

*All respond:*

Blessed be God for ever.

*Then the Scripture is read:*

Listen to the words of the book of Job:

So I have been assigned months of misery,
    and troubled nights have been told off for me.

If in bed I say, "When shall I arise?"
    Then the night drags on;
    I am filled with restlessness until the dawn.
My flesh is clothed with worms and scabs;
    my skin cracks and festers;
My days are swifter than a weaver's shuttle;
    they come to an end without hope.
Remember that my life is like the wind;
    I shall not see happiness again.

My own utterance I will not restrain;
    I will speak in the anguish of my spirit;
    I will complain in the bitterness of my soul.

Job 7:3-7,11

*The reader concludes:*

This is the Word of the Lord.

*All respond:*

Thanks be to God.

*After a time of silence, all join in prayers of
intercession and in the Lord's Prayer. Then the
leader prays:*

God of all mercies, God of all consolation,
comfort us in our afflictions
that we in turn might comfort those who are in
   trouble
with the same consolation we have received.

Grant this through Christ our Lord.
R. Amen.

*The leader concludes:*

Let us bless the Lord.

*All respond, making the sign of the cross:*

Thanks be to God.

*The blessing may conclude with "Amazing Grace"*
*(page 318) or another appropriate song.*


*Prayers in times of family strife:*

A    God of compassion and grace,
     in your steadfast love accompany N. and N.
     As you ever work to restore and renew your
        people,
     overcome bitterness with your joy,
     hatred with your love, brokenness with your
        life;
     and give us hope
     through the death and resurrection of your
        Son,
     Jesus Christ our Lord.
     R. Amen.

**B**  O God, you have bound us together in a common life.
Help us in the midst of our struggles
to confront one another without hatred or bitterness,
and to work together with mutual forbearance and respect.

We ask this through Jesus Christ our Lord.
R. Amen.

*Prayer in time of neighborhood or racial strife:*

O God, the Lord of all,
your Son commanded us to love our enemies
and to pray for them.
Lead us from prejudice to truth;
deliver us from hatred, cruelty, and revenge;
and enable us to stand before you,
reconciled through your Son, Jesus Christ our Lord.
R. Amen.

# BLESSING IN TIMES OF PENANCE AND RECONCILIATION

On Fridays, on various other days appointed through the year, and especially during the season of Lent, the whole Church is called to penance: to turn away from evil and to seek reconciliation with God and one another in prayer and in deeds. Prayers for Fridays are found on page 193, for Ember Days on page 186, and for Lent on page 137. Prayers for the sacrament of penance are on page 248. The following may be appropriate when the household needs to express sorrow over past deeds and to make peace. Works of kindness and of justice should accompany such prayer.

*All make the sign of the cross. The leader begins:*

Let us come with confidence before the throne of
    grace
to receive God's mercy,
and we shall find pardon and strength in our
    time of need.
Blessed be God for ever.

*All respond:*

Blessed be God for ever.

*Then the Scripture is read. Any appropriate
reading may be selected. The following examples
should not limit the choice.*

A   Listen to the words of the prophet Isaiah:

Hear, O heavens, and listen, O earth,
   for the LORD speaks:

When you spread out your hands,
   I close my eyes to you;
Though you pray the more,
   I will not listen.
Your hands are full of blood!
   Wash yourselves clean!

Put away your misdeeds from before my eyes;
   cease doing evil; learn to do good.
Make justice your aim: redress the wronged,
   hear the orphan's plea, defend the widow.

Come now, let us set things right, says the Lord:
Though your sins be like scarlet,
   they may become white as snow;
Though they be crimson red,
   they may become white as wool.

Isaiah 1:2,15-18

Or:

B   Listen to the words of the first letter of John:

If we say, "We have fellowship with [God],"
while we continue to walk in darkness, we lie
and do not act in truth.

My children, I am writing this to you so that you
may not commit sin. But if anyone does sin, we

have an Advocate with the Father, Jesus Christ
the righteous one. He is expiation for our sins,
and not for our sins only but for those of the
whole world.

1 John 1:6; 2:1-2

*The reader concludes:*

This is the Word of the Lord.

*All respond:*

Thanks be to God.

*After a time of silence, all kneel. The leader may
begin:*

We may now speak of the wrong we have done
and the good we have not done. Let us ask
forgiveness of one another, of others, and of
God.

*After this, all may join in the Confiteor (page
91) or the Act of Contrition (page 250). There
may then be prayers of intercession. All stand and
join hands for the Lord's Prayer. The leader then
prays:*

Loving God, our source of life,
you know our weakness.
May we reach out with joy to grasp your hand
and walk more readily in your ways.

We ask this through Christ our Lord.
R. Amen.

*All make the sign of the cross as the leader concludes:*

May God, who frees us from sin,
bless us and keep us always in peace.
R. Amen.

*The blessing may conclude with the exchange of peace and with an appropriate song such as "The Old Hundreth" (Praise God from Whom All Blessings Flow) (page 324) or the following:*

Amazing grace! how sweet the sound,
That saved a wretch like me!
I once was lost, but now am found,
Was blind, but now I see.

'Twas grace that taught my heart to fear,
And grace my fears relieved;
How precious did that grace appear
The hour I first believed!

The Lord has promised good to me,
God's word my hope secures;
God will my shield and portion be
As long as life endures.

Through many dangers, toils and snares,
I have already come;
'Tis grace has brought me safe thus far,
And grace will lead me home.

John Newton

*The following prayer is appropriate for Advent:*

All around us, Lord, and within us too
there is emptiness.
We have grown weary pursuing justice,
despaired of peace that is so hard and slow.
Often we do not even know what we need
for ours is an emptiness made of haste.

But our hearts would exult simply to hear your
   voice.
How we would stand straight
and fill ourselves with your word!

We wait for your Messiah,
keeping watch and praying in his name,
Jesus, who is Lord for ever and ever.
R. Amen.

*The following may be sung during Lent:*

Kind Maker of the world, O hear
The fervent prayer, with many a tear
Poured forth by all the penitent
Who keep this holy fast of Lent.

Each heart is manifest to thee;
Thou knowest our infirmity;
Now we repent, and seek thy face;
Grant unto us thy pardoning grace.

Spare us, O Lord, who now confess
Our sins and all our wickedness,
And, for the glory of thy Name,
Our weakened souls to health reclaim.

Give us the discipline that springs
From abstinence in outward things
With inward fasting, so that we
In heart and soul may dwell with thee.

Grant, O thou blessed Trinity,
Grant, O unchanging Unity,
That this our fast of forty days
May work our profit and thy praise.

*Gregory the Great*

## PRAYER IN TIMES OF SEEKING GOD'S WILL

When important decisions are to be made, the following psalm may be a part of the table prayer, or may be used at another time. "Come, Holy Spirit" (page 157) is also appropriate.

Hear, O LORD, the sound of my call;
   have pity on me, and answer me.
Of you my heart speaks; you my glance seeks;
   your presence, O LORD, I seek.
Hide not your face from me;
   do not in anger repel your servant.
You are my helper: cast me not off;
   forsake me not, O God my savior.

I believe that I shall see the bounty of the LORD
  in the land of the living.
Wait for the LORD with courage;
  be stouthearted, and wait for the LORD.

Psalm 27:7-9,13-14

# BLESSING TO BE USED IN VARIOUS CIRCUMSTANCES

This blessing may be adapted to various circumstances not explicitly provided for elsewhere in this book. It is not meant to be used in inappropriate ways (the blessing of weapons or of frivolous events, for example).

*All make the sign of the cross. The leader begins:*

Let us bless and praise the Lord, the fountain of all goodness. Blessed be God for ever.

*All respond:*

Blessed be God for ever.

*The leader may use these or similar words to introduce the blessing:*

All that God has created and sustains, all the events he guides, and all human works that are good and have a good purpose, prompt those who believe to praise and bless the Lord with hearts and voices. God is the source and origin of every blessing. By this celebration, we proclaim our belief that all things work together for the good of those who fear and love God. We are sure that in all things, we must seek the help of God, so that in complete reliance on his will we may, in Christ, do everything for his glory.

*Then the Scripture is read:*

Listen to the words of the apostle Paul to Timothy:

Everything created by God is good, and nothing is to be rejected when received with thanksgiving, for it is made holy by the invocation of God in prayer.

1 Timothy 4:4-5

*(The family's Bible may be used for an alternate reading such as Colossians 1:9-14; Romans 8:24-28; Numbers 6:22-27; Deuteronomy 33:1,13-16; Wisdom 13:1-7; Sirach 18:1-9; or other texts as suggested by the occasion.)*

*The reader concludes:*

This is the Word of the Lord.

*All respond:*

Thanks be to God.

*After a time of silence, all join in prayers of intercession and in the Lord's Prayer. Then the leader speaks the blessing:*

## BLESSING FOR THE PRODUCTS OF NATURE

Blessed are you, O God,
Creator of the universe,
who have made all things good
and given the earth for us to cultivate.
Grant that we may always use created things
   gratefully
and share your gifts with those in need,
out of the love of Christ our Lord,
who lives and reigns with you for ever and ever.
R. Amen.

## BLESSING FOR THE PRODUCTS OF HUMAN LABOR

Almighty and ever-living God,
you have made us stewards over the created
   world,
so that in all things we might honor the demands
   of charity.
Graciously hear our prayers,
that your blessing may come upon all those
who use these objects for their needs.
Let them always see you as the good surpassing
   every good
and love their neighbor with upright hearts.

We ask this through Christ our Lord.
R. Amen.

## BLESSING FOR THE SPECIAL OCCASIONS OF LIFE

Lord God,
from the abundance of your mercy
enrich your servants and safeguard them.
Strengthened by your blessing,
may they always be thankful to you
and bless you with unending joy.

We ask this through Christ our Lord.
R. Amen.

*All make the sign of the cross as the leader concludes:*

May God, who is blessed above all,
bless us in all things through Christ,
so that whatever happens in our lives
will work together for our good.
R. Amen.

*The blessing may conclude with song:*

Praise God from whom all blessings flow,
Praise God all creatures here below,
Praise God above, ye heav'nly host:
Praise Father, Son and Holy Ghost.

# PART V
# COMMON PRAYERS

# INTRODUCTION

Some of our most familiar prayers are included within the various blessings in the previous sections. Others will be found in the following pages. These also form part of the daily or seasonal rites of the individual Christian and of the household. Also given here are prayers in languages that the Church has treasured in the past: Hebrew, Aramaic, Greek, and Latin.

# PRAYERS OF INTERCESSION

All who are baptized are charged to offer constant prayer to God for the world, the Church, the poor, all in need, and those who have died. This intercession is a part of morning and evening prayer and of the Sunday eucharist. These texts are examples of ways the Church has made intercession.

## 1. PRAYER FOR ALL NEEDS

We beg you, Lord,
to help and defend us.

Deliver the oppressed.
Pity the insignificant.
Raise the fallen.
Show yourself to the needy.
Heal the sick.
Bring back those of your people who have gone
    astray.
Feed the hungry.
Lift up the weak.
Take off the prisoners' chains.

May every nation come to know
that you alone are God,
that Jesus is your Child,
that we are your people, the sheep that you
    pasture.
R. Amen.

Clement of Rome

## 2. EVENING INTERCESSIONS

In peace, let us pray to the Lord.

R. Lord have mercy.

For an evening that is perfect, holy, peaceful, and without sin, let us pray to the Lord.

For an angel of peace, a faithful guide, and guardian of our souls and bodies, let us pray to the Lord.

For the pardon and forgiveness of our sins and offenses, let us pray to the Lord.

For the holy Church of God, that God may give it peace and unity and protect and prosper it throughout the whole world, let us pray to the Lord.

For this nation, its government and all who serve and protect us, let us pray to the Lord.

For this city (town, village) of N. and for every city and land and for all those living in them, let us pray to the Lord.

For seasonable weather, bountiful harvests, and for peaceful times, let us pray to the Lord.

For the safety of travelers, the recovery of the sick, the deliverance of the oppressed, and the release of captives, let us pray to the Lord.

For all that is good and profitable to our souls and for the peace of the world, let us pray to the Lord.

For a peaceful and Christian end to our lives without shame or pain, and for a good defense before the awesome judgment seat of Christ, let us pray to the Lord.

Help, save, pity, and defend us, O God, by your grace.

> (*Pause for silent prayer and/or additional petitions.*)

Rejoicing in the communion of the Blessed Virgin Mary and of all the saints, let us commend ourselves and one another to the living God through Christ our Lord.

R. To you, O Lord.

Ancient Byzantine Litany

## 3. OTHER INTERCESSIONS

For the peace of the world, that a spirit of respect and forbearance may grow among nations and peoples, let us pray to the Lord.

For the holy Church of God, that it may be filled with truth and love and be found without fault at the day of your coming, let us pray to the Lord.

For those in positions of public trust, (especially
_____), that they may serve justice and
promote the dignity and freedom of all people,
let us pray to the Lord.

For a blessing upon the labors of all, and for the
right use of the riches of creation, let us pray to
the Lord.

For the poor, the persecuted, the sick, and all
who suffer; for refugees, prisoners, and all who
are in danger, that they may be relieved and
protected, let us pray to the Lord.

For this household; for those who are present,
and for those who are absent, that we may be
delivered from hardness of heart and show forth
your glory in all that we do, let us pray to the
Lord.

For our enemies and those who wish us harm;
and for all whom we have injured or offended,
let us pray to the Lord.

For all who have died in the faith of Christ, that
with all the saints, they may have rest in that
place where there is no pain or grief, but life
eternal, let us pray to the Lord.

*Ancient Byzantine Litany*


## 4. SHORTER INTERCESSIONS

Let us pray to God who cares for all, and with
earnest humility say:
R. Have mercy on your people, Lord.

Guard the Church.

Watch over N., our Pope.

Protect and bless N., our bishop.

Save your people.

Preserve peace among the nations.

Bring an end to strife and hatred.

Guide the rulers of nations.

Guide parents in the fulfillment of their responsibilities.

Nourish children by your loving care.

Support and give solace to the aged.

Be a helper to the poor.

Comfort those who are troubled.

Grant deliverance to captives.

Bring exiles back to their homeland.

Grant health to the sick.

Be present to those who are dying.

Admit those who have died into the company of the saints.

*Liturgy of the Hours*

# PRAYERS OF PRAISE AND THANKSGIVING

Praise and thanksgiving are frequently woven together in Christian prayer. This is seen most clearly in the eucharistic prayer. Prayers of praise and/or thanksgiving found elsewhere in this book include: "Glory to the Father" (page 25); "Glory to God in the Highest" (page 26); "Praise God from Whom All Blessings Flow" (page 324); "Now Thank We All Our God" (page 291).

The *Te Deum* (meaning, "You are God") is a fourth century hymn that became the Church's great song of thanksgiving. "Holy God, We Praise Thy Name" is an English paraphrase of the *Te Deum*. The Divine Praises is a litany in which God is blessed over and over for the mystery of our salvation.

### 5. TE DEUM

You are God: we praise you;
You are the Lord: we acclaim you;
You are the eternal Father:
All creation worships you.

To you all angels, all the powers of heaven,
Cherubim and Seraphim, sing in endless praise:
  Holy, holy, holy Lord, God of power and
  might,
  heaven and earth are full of your glory.

The glorious company of apostles praise you.
The noble fellowship of prophets praise you.
The white-robed army of martyrs praise you.

Throughout the world the holy Church acclaims
    you:
    Father, of majesty unbounded,
your true and only Son, worthy of all worship,
    and the Holy Spirit, advocate and guide.

You, Christ, are the king of glory,
the eternal Son of the Father.

When you became man to set us free
you did not spurn the Virgin's womb.

You overcame the sting of death,
and opened the kingdom of heaven to all
    believers.

You are seated at God's right hand in glory.
We believe that you will come, and be our judge.
    Come then, Lord, and help your people,
    bought with the price of your own blood,
    and bring us with your saints
    to glory everlasting.


## 6. HOLY GOD, WE PRAISE THY NAME

Holy God, we praise thy name!
Lord of all, we bow before thee;
All on earth thy scepter claim,
All in heav'n above adore thee;
Infinite thy vast domain,
Everlasting is thy reign.

Hark! the loud celestial hymn
Angel choirs above are raising;
Cherubim and Seraphim
In unceasing chorus praising,
Fill the heav'ns with the sweet accord:
Holy, holy, holy Lord!

Lo! the apostolic train
Join the sacred Name to hallow;
Prophets swell the loud refrain,
And the white-robed martyrs follow;
And from morn to set of sun,
Through the Church the song goes on.

Holy Father, Holy Son,
Holy Spirit, Three we name thee,
While in essence only One,
Undivided God we claim thee,
And adoring bend the knee,
While we own the mystery.

## 7. THE DIVINE PRAISES

Blessed be God.
Blessed be his holy name.
Blessed be Jesus Christ, true God and true man.
Blessed be the name of Jesus.
Blessed be his most sacred heart.
Blessed be his most precious blood.
Blessed be Jesus in the most holy sacrament of
    the altar.
Blessed be the Holy Spirit, the Paraclete.
Blessed be the great mother of God, Mary most
    holy.
Blessed be her holy and immaculate conception.

Blessed be her glorious assumption.
Blessed be the name of Mary, virgin and mother.
Blessed be Saint Joseph, her most chaste spouse.
Blessed be God in his angels and in his saints.

# LITANIES

The litany is a way of praying found among many peoples. It is a prayer made to be repeated: one phrase coming over and over again so that the person praying is caught up in the prayer itself. Often litanies are chanted.

The Litanies of the Holy Name, of the Sacred Heart, of the Blessed Virgin Mary (called the Litany of Loreto), and of Saint Joseph took shape over several centuries. All four are rooted in images we find in the Scriptures. The Litany of the Saints is part of the Church's liturgy on many occasions (baptism and ordination, for example). It may be lengthened to include the names of other saints.

## 8. LITANY OF THE HOLY NAME

| | |
|---|---|
| Lord, have mercy | Lord, have mercy |
| Christ, have mercy | Christ, have mercy |
| Lord, have mercy | Lord, have mercy |
| | |
| God our Father in heaven | have mercy on us |
| God the Son, Redeemer of the world | have mercy on us |

| | |
|---|---|
| God the Holy Spirit | have mercy on us |
| Holy Trinity, one God | have mercy on us |
| Jesus, Son of the living God | have mercy on us |
| Jesus, splendor of the Father | have mercy on us |
| Jesus, brightness of everlasting light | have mercy on us |
| Jesus, king of glory | have mercy on us |
| Jesus, dawn of justice | have mercy on us |
| Jesus, Son of the Virgin Mary | have mercy on us |
| Jesus, worthy of our love | have mercy on us |
| Jesus, worthy of our wonder | have mercy on us |
| Jesus, mighty God | have mercy on us |
| Jesus, father of the world to come | have mercy on us |
| Jesus, prince of peace | have mercy on us |
| Jesus, all-powerful | have mercy on us |
| Jesus, pattern of patience | have mercy on us |
| Jesus, model of obedience | have mercy on us |
| Jesus, gentle and humble of heart | have mercy on us |
| Jesus, lover of chastity | have mercy on us |
| Jesus, lover of us all | have mercy on us |
| Jesus, God of peace | have mercy on us |
| Jesus, author of life | have mercy on us |
| Jesus, model of goodness | have mercy on us |
| Jesus, seeker of souls | have mercy on us |

| | |
|---|---|
| Jesus, our God | have mercy on us |
| Jesus, our refuge | have mercy on us |
| Jesus, father of the poor | have mercy on us |
| Jesus, treasure of the faithful | have mercy on us |
| | |
| Jesus, Good Shepherd | have mercy on us |
| Jesus, the true light | have mercy on us |
| Jesus, eternal wisdom | have mercy on us |
| Jesus, infinite goodness | have mercy on us |
| Jesus, our way and our life | have mercy on us |
| Jesus, joy of angels | have mercy on us |
| Jesus, king of patriarchs | have mercy on us |
| Jesus, teacher of apostles | have mercy on us |
| Jesus, master of evangelists | have mercy on us |
| Jesus, courage of martyrs | have mercy on us |
| Jesus, light of confessors | have mercy on us |
| Jesus, purity of virgins | have mercy on us |
| Jesus, crown of all saints | have mercy on us |
| | |
| Lord, be merciful | Jesus, save your people |
| From all evil | Jesus, save your people |
| From every sin | Jesus, save your people |
| From the snares of the devil | Jesus, save your people |

| | |
|---|---|
| From your anger | Jesus, save your people |
| From the spirit of infidelity | Jesus, save your people |
| From everlasting death | Jesus, save your people |
| From neglect of your Holy Spirit | Jesus, save your people |
| By the mystery of your incarnation | Jesus, save your people |
| By your birth | Jesus, save your people |
| By your childhood | Jesus, save your people |
| By your hidden life | Jesus, save your people |
| By your public ministry | Jesus, save your people |
| By your agony and crucifixion | Jesus, save your people |
| By your abandonment | Jesus, save your people |
| By your grief and sorrow | Jesus, save your people |
| By your death and burial | Jesus, save your people |
| By your rising to new life | Jesus, save your people |
| By your return in glory to the Father | Jesus, save your people |
| By your gift of the holy eucharist | Jesus, save your people |
| By your joy and glory | Jesus, save your people |

Christize, hear us     Christ, hear us
Lord Jesus, hear our     Lord Jesus, hear our
    prayer             prayer

Lamb of God, you take
    away the sins of the
    world               have mercy on us
Lamb of God, you take
    away the sins of the
    world               have mercy on us
Lamb of God, you take
    away the sins of the
    world               have mercy on us

Let us pray.

Lord,
may we who honor the holy name of Jesus
enjoy his friendship in this life
and be filled with eternal joy in the kingdom
where he lives and reigns for ever and ever.
R. Amen.


## 9. LITANY OF THE SACRED HEART


Lord, have mercy     Lord, have mercy
Christ, have mercy     Christ, have mercy
Lord, have mercy     Lord, have mercy

God our Father in
    heaven              have mercy on us
God the Son, Redeemer
    of the world        have mercy on us
God the Holy Spirit     have mercy on us

| | |
|---|---|
| Holy Trinity, one God | have mercy on us |
| Heart of Jesus, Son of the eternal Father | have mercy on us |
| Heart of Jesus, formed by the Holy Spirit in the womb of the Virgin Mother | have mercy on us |
| Heart of Jesus, one with the eternal Word | have mercy on us |
| Heart of Jesus, infinite in majesty | have mercy on us |
| Heart of Jesus, holy temple of God | have mercy on us |
| Heart of Jesus, tabernacle of the Most High | have mercy on us |
| Heart of Jesus, house of God and gate of heaven | have mercy on us |
| Heart of Jesus, aflame with love for us | have mercy on us |
| Heart of Jesus, source of justice and love | have mercy on us |
| Heart of Jesus, full of goodness and love | have mercy on us |
| Heart of Jesus, well-spring of all virtue | have mercy on us |
| Heart of Jesus, worthy of all praise | have mercy on us |
| Heart of Jesus, king and center of all hearts | have mercy on us |

| | |
|---|---|
| Heart of Jesus, treasure-house of wisdom and knowledge | have mercy on us |
| Heart of Jesus, in whom there dwells the fullness of God | have mercy on us |
| Heart of Jesus, in whom the Father is well pleased | have mercy on us |
| Heart of Jesus, from whose fullness we have all received | have mercy on us |
| Heart of Jesus, desire of the eternal hills | have mercy on us |
| Heart of Jesus, patient and full of mercy | have mercy on us |
| Heart of Jesus, generous to all who turn to you | have mercy on us |
| Heart of Jesus, fountain of life and holiness | have mercy on us |
| Heart of Jesus, atonement for our sins | have mercy on us |
| Heart of Jesus, overwhelmed with insults | have mercy on us |
| Heart of Jesus, broken for our sins | have mercy on us |
| Heart of Jesus, obedient even to death | have mercy on us |
| Heart of Jesus, pierced by a lance | have mercy on us |

| | |
|---|---|
| Heart of Jesus, source of all consolation | have mercy on us |
| Heart of Jesus, our life and resurrection | have mercy on us |
| Heart of Jesus, our peace and reconciliation | have mercy on us |
| Heart of Jesus, victim for our sins | have mercy on us |
| Heart of Jesus, salvation of all who trust in you | have mercy on us |
| Heart of Jesus, hope of all who die in you | have mercy on us |
| Heart of Jesus, delight of all the saints | have mercy on us |
| Lamb of God, you take away the sins of the world | have mercy on us |
| Lamb of God, you take away the sins of the world | have mercy on us |
| Lamb of God, you take away the sins of the world | have mercy on us |

V. Jesus, gentle and humble of heart.

R. Touch our hearts and make them like your own.

Let us pray.

Father,
we rejoice in the gifts of love
we have received from the heart of Jesus
   your Son.
Open our hearts to share his life
and continue to bless us with his love.
We ask this in the name of Jesus the Lord.
R. Amen.

## 10. LITANY OF THE BLESSED VIRGIN MARY

Lord, have mercy         Lord, have mercy
Christ, have mercy       Christ, have mercy
Lord, have mercy         Lord, have mercy

God our Father in
   heaven             have mercy on us
God the Son, Redeemer
   of the world       have mercy on us
God the Holy Spirit      have mercy on us
Holy Trinity, one God    have mercy on us

Holy Mary            pray for us
Holy Mother of God     pray for us
Most honored of
   virgins            pray for us

Mother of Christ        pray for us
Mother of the Church    pray for us
Mother of divine grace   pray for us
Mother most pure       pray for us
Mother of chaste love    pray for us
Mother and virgin       pray for us
Sinless Mother         pray for us

| | |
|---|---|
| Dearest of mothers | pray for us |
| Model of motherhood | pray for us |
| Mother of good counsel | pray for us |
| Mother of our Creator | pray for us |
| Mother of our Savior | pray for us |
| Virgin most wise | pray for us |
| Virgin rightly praised | pray for us |
| Virgin rightly renowned | pray for us |
| Virgin most powerful | pray for us |
| Virgin gentle in mercy | pray for us |
| Faithful Virgin | pray for us |
| Mirror of justice | pray for us |
| Throne of wisdom | pray for us |
| Cause of our joy | pray for us |
| | |
| Shrine of the Spirit | pray for us |
| Glory of Israel | pray for us |
| Vessel of selfless devotion | pray for us |
| Mystical Rose | pray for us |
| Tower of David | pray for us |
| Tower of ivory | pray for us |
| House of gold | pray for us |
| Ark of the covenant | pray for us |
| Gate of heaven | pray for us |
| Morning Star | pray for us |
| Health of the sick | pray for us |
| Refuge of sinners | pray for us |
| Comfort of the troubled | pray for us |
| Help of Christians | pray for us |
| | |
| Queen of angels | pray for us |
| Queen of patriarchs and prophets | pray for us |

| | |
|---|---|
| Queen of apostles and<br>    martyrs | pray for us |
| Queen of confessors<br>    and virgins | pray for us |
| Queen of all saints | pray for us |
| Queen conceived<br>    without sin | pray for us |
| Queen assumed into<br>    heaven | pray for us |
| Queen of the rosary | pray for us |
| Queen of peace | pray for us |

| | |
|---|---|
| Lamb of God, you take<br>    away the sins of the<br>    world | have mercy on us |
| Lamb of God, you take<br>    away the sins of the<br>    world | have mercy on us |
| Lamb of God, you take<br>    away the sins of the<br>    world | have mercy on us |

V. Pray for us, holy Mother of God.
R. That we may become worthy of the promises
    of Christ.

Let us pray.

Eternal God,
let your people enjoy constant health in mind
    and body.
Through the intercession of the Virgin Mary
free us from the sorrows of this life
and lead us to happiness in the life to come.
Grant this through Christ our Lord.
R. Amen.

## 11. LITANY OF SAINT JOSEPH

| | |
|---|---|
| Lord, have mercy | Lord, have mercy |
| Christ, have mercy | Christ, have mercy |
| Holy Trinity, one God | have mercy on us |
| | |
| Holy Mary | pray for us |
| | |
| Saint Joseph | pray for us |
| Noble son of the House of David | pray for us |
| Light of patriarchs | pray for us |
| Husband of the Mother of God | pray for us |
| Guardian of the Virgin | pray for us |
| Foster father of the Son of God | pray for us |
| Faithful guardian of Christ | pray for us |
| Head of the holy family | pray for us |
| Joseph, chaste and just | pray for us |
| Joseph, prudent and brave | pray for us |
| Joseph, obedient and loyal | pray for us |
| Pattern of patience | pray for us |
| Lover of poverty | pray for us |
| Model of workers | pray for us |
| Example to parents | pray for us |
| Guardian of virgins | pray for us |
| Pillar of family life | pray for us |

| | |
|---|---|
| Comfort of the troubled | pray for us |
| Hope of the sick | pray for us |
| Patron of the dying | pray for us |
| Terror of evil spirits | pray for us |
| Protector of the Church | pray for us |

| | |
|---|---|
| Lamb of God, you take away the sins of the world | have mercy on us |
| Lamb of God, you take away the sins of the world | have mercy on us |
| Lamb of God, you take away the sins of the world | have mercy on us |

V. God made him master of his household.
R. And put him in charge of all that he owned.

Let us pray.

Almighty God,
in your infinite wisdom and love
you chose Joseph to be the husband of Mary,
the mother of your Son.
As we enjoy his protection on earth
may we have the help of his prayers in heaven.

We ask this through Christ our Lord.
R. Amen.

## 12. LITANY OF THE SAINTS

| | |
|---|---|
| Lord, have mercy | Lord, have mercy |
| Christ, have mercy | Christ, have mercy |
| Lord, have mercy | Lord, have mercy |
| Holy Mary, Mother of God | pray for us |
| Saint Michael | pray for us |
| Holy angels of God | pray for us |
| Saint John the Baptist | pray for us |
| Saint Joseph | pray for us |
| Saint Peter and Saint Paul | pray for us |
| Saint Andrew | pray for us |
| Saint John | pray for us |
| Saint Mary Magdalene | pray for us |
| Saint Stephen | pray for us |
| Saint Ignatius of Antioch | pray for us |
| Saint Lawrence | pray for us |
| Saint Perpetua and Saint Felicity | pray for us |
| Saint Agnes | pray for us |
| Saint Gregory | pray for us |
| Saint Augustine | pray for us |
| Saint Athanasius | pray for us |
| Saint Basil | pray for us |
| Saint Martin | pray for us |
| Saint Benedict | pray for us |
| Saint Francis and Saint Dominic | pray for us |
| Saint Francis Xavier | pray for us |
| Saint John Vianney | pray for us |

| | |
|---|---|
| Saint Catherine | pray for us |
| Saint Teresa | pray for us |
| *(Other names of saints may be added.)* | (pray for us) |
| All holy men and women | pray for us |
| Lord, be merciful | Lord, save your people |
| From all evil | Lord, save your people |
| From every sin | Lord, save your people |
| From everlasting death | Lord, save your people |
| By your coming as man | Lord, save your people |
| By your death and rising to new life | Lord, save your people |
| By your gift of the Holy Spirit | Lord, save your people |
| Be merciful to us sinners | Lord, hear our prayer |
| Guide and protect your holy Church | Lord, hear our prayer |
| Keep the pope and all the clergy in faithful service to your Church | Lord, hear our prayer |
| Bring all peoples together in trust and peace | Lord, hear our prayer |

| | |
|---|---|
| Strengthen us in your service | Lord, hear our prayer |
| Jesus, Son of the living God | Lord, hear our prayer |
| Christ, hear us | Christ, hear us |
| Lord Jesus, hear our prayer | Lord Jesus, hear our prayer |

Let us pray.

God of our ancestors who set their hearts on you,
of those who fell asleep in peace,
and of those who won the martyrs' violent
    crown:
We are surrounded by these witnesses
as by clouds of fragrant incense.
In this age we would be counted
in this communion of all the saints;
keep us always in their good and blessed
    company.
In their midst we make every prayer
through Christ who is our Lord for ever and
    ever.
R. Amen.

# PSALMS AND CANTICLES

The psalms are the basic prayer texts of Jews and Christians. For the Church, they are the core of daily prayer. At Sunday eucharist the psalms are the song and reflection of the assembly. The Psalter—the Bible's collection of 150 psalms—is our prayerbook and the touchstone of all our other prayers.

Elsewhere in this book, several psalms are given in part or in their entirety: Psalm 23 ("The Lord is my shepherd," page 282); Psalm 51 (the Miserere, page 29); Psalm 95 (a call to worship, page 34); Psalm 102 (page 62); Psalm 121 (page 242); Psalm 148 (page 33). Together with these, the following psalms make an introduction and invitation to the whole psalter. In some traditions, the prayer "Glory to the Father" is recited at the conclusion of a psalm.

Canticles are psalm-like texts that occur outside the Book of Psalms. Christians pray each morning the Benedictus or Canticle of Zechariah (page 30); each evening the Magnificat or Canticle of Mary (page 48); each night the Nunc Dimittis or Canticle of Simeon (page 92). All three are found in the gospel of Luke; all are filled with the images of older psalms and canticles from the Hebrew Scriptures. Two canticles from the Hebrew Scriptures and one from the New Testament are given below.

## 13. PSALM 91

*A lenten and night psalm.*

You who dwell in the shelter of the Most High,
    who abide in the shadow of the Almighty,
Say to the LORD, "My refuge and my fortress,
    my God, in whom I trust."
For he will rescue you from the snare of the
    fowler,
    from the destroying pestilence.
With his pinions he will cover you,
    and under his wings you shall take refuge;
    his faithfulness is a buckler and a shield.
You shall not fear the terror of the night
    nor the arrow that flies by day;
Not the pestilence that roams in darkness
    nor the devastating plague at noon.
Though a thousand fall at your side,
    ten thousand at your right side,
    near you it shall not come.
Rather with your eyes shall you behold
    and see the requital of the wicked,
Because you have the LORD for your refuge;
    you have made the Most High your
    stronghold.
No evil shall befall you,
    nor shall affliction come near your tent,
For to his angels he has given command about
    you,
    that they guard you in all your ways.
Upon their hands they shall bear you up,
    lest you dash your foot against a stone.
You shall tread upon the asp and the viper;
    you shall trample down the lion and the
    dragon.

Because he clings to me, I will deliver him;
    I will set him on high because he acknowledges
    my name.
He shall call upon me, and I will answer him;
    I will be with him in distress;
I will deliver him and glorify him;
    with length of days I will gratify him
    and will show him my salvation.

## 14. PSALM 100

*A song of praise; a morning prayer.*

Sing joyfully to the LORD, all you lands;
    serve the Lord with gladness;
    come before him with joyful song.
Know that the LORD is God;
    he made us, his we are;
    his people, the flock he tends.
Enter his gates with thanksgiving,
    his courts with praise;
Give thanks to him; bless his name, for he is
    good:
    the Lord, whose kindness endures forever,
    and his faithfulness, to all generations.

## 15. PSALM 130

*In difficult times.*

Out of the depths I cry to you, O LORD;
    LORD, hear my voice!
Let your ears be attentive
    to my voice in supplication:

If you, O LORD, mark iniquities,
    LORD, who can stand?
But with you is forgiveness,
    that you may be revered.

I trust in the LORD;
    my soul trusts in his word.
My soul waits for the LORD
    more than sentinels wait for the dawn.

More than sentinels wait for the dawn,
    let Israel wait for the LORD,
For with the LORD is kindness
    and with him is plenteous redemption;
And he will redeem Israel
    from all their iniquities.

## 16. PSALM 141

*An evening psalm of repentance.*

O LORD, to you I call; hasten to me;
    hearken to my voice when I call upon you.
Let my prayer come like incense before you;
    the lifting up of my hands, like the evening
    sacrifice.

O LORD, set a watch before my mouth,
    a guard at the door of my lips.
Let not my heart incline to the evil
    of engaging in deeds of wickedness
With men who are evildoers;
    and let me not partake of their dainties.
Let the just man strike me; that is kindness;
    let him reprove me; it is oil for the head,

Which my head shall not refuse,
   but I will still pray under these afflictions.
Their judges were cast down over the crag,
   and they heard how pleasant were my words.
As when a plowman breaks furrows in the field,
   so their bones are strewn by the edge of the
   nether world.

For toward you, O GOD, my Lord, my eyes are
   turned;
   in you I take refuge; strip me not of life.
Keep me from the trap they have set for me,
   and from the snares of evildoers.
Let all the wicked fall, each into his own net,
   while I escape.

## 17. PSALM 150

*The hymn of praise which concludes the psalter.*

Praise the LORD in his sanctuary,
   praise him in the firmament of his strength.
Praise him for his mighty deeds,
   praise him for his sovereign majesty.
Praise him with the blast of the trumpet,
   praise him with lyre and harp,
Praise him with timbrel and dance,
   praise him with strings and pipe.
Praise him with sounding cymbals,
   praise him with clanging cymbals.
Let everything that has breath
   praise the LORD! Alleluia.

## 18. A CANTICLE OF ISAIAH

*Rejoicing in God our Mother.*

Rejoice with Jerusalem and be glad because of
    her,
    all you who love her;
Exult, exult with her,
    all you who were mourning over her!
Oh, that you may suck fully
    of the milk of her comfort,
That you may nurse with delight
    at her abundant breasts!
For thus says the Lord:
Lo, I will spread prosperity over her like a river,
    and the wealth of the nations like an
    overflowing torrent.
As nurslings, you shall be carried in her arms,
    and fondled in her lap;
As a mother comforts her [child],
    so will I comfort you;
    in Jerusalem you shall find your comfort.

Isaiah 66:10-13

## 19. A CANTICLE OF JEREMIAH

*Return to the Lord, the only God.*

Let my eyes stream with tears
    day and night, without rest,
Over the great destruction which overwhelms
    the virgin daughter of my people,
    over her incurable wound.

If I walk out into the field,
   look! those slain by the sword;
If I enter the city,
   look! those consumed by hunger.
Even the prophet and the priest
   forage in a land they know not.

Have you cast Judah off completely?
   Is Zion loathsome to you?
Why have you struck us a blow
   that cannot be healed?
We wait for peace, to no avail;
   for a time of healing, but terror comes instead.

We recognize, O LORD, our wickedness,
   the guilt of our fathers;
   that we have sinned against you.

For your name's sake spurn us not,
   disgrace not the throne of your glory;
   remember your covenant with us, and break it
   not.

Among the nations' idols is there any that gives
   rain?
   Or can the mere heavens send showers?
Is it not you alone, O LORD,
   our God, to whom we look?
You alone have done all these things.

                                        Jeremiah 14:17-21

## 20. A CANTICLE FROM PHILIPPIANS

*An ancient Christian hymn.*

Though [Christ] was in the form of God,
  [he] did not regard equality with God
    something to be grasped.
Rather, he emptied himself
  taking the form of a slave,
  coming in human likeness;
  and found human in appearance,
  he humbled himself,
  becoming obedient to death,
    even death on a cross.
Because of this, God greatly exalted him
  and bestowed on him the name
  that is above every name,
  that at the name of Jesus
  every knee should bend,
  of those in heaven and on earth
    and under the earth,
  and every tongue confess that
  Jesus Christ is Lord,
  to the glory of God the Father.

Philippians 2:6-11

# THE HOLY EUCHARIST

In addition to the eucharistic prayers of the Mass and the texts of the communion rite, the Church has many prayers that are appropriate before and after holy communion. Most of these, like the ones given below, date from the twelfth century or later. See also "How holy this feast" on page 106. The last two verses of the "Pange Lingua" are often referred to as the "Tantum ergo."

## 21. ANIMA CHRISTI

Soul of Christ, sanctify me.
Body of Christ, heal me.
Blood of Christ, drench me.
Water from the side of Christ, wash me.
Passion of Christ, strengthen me.

Good Jesus, hear me.

In your wounds shelter me.
From turning away keep me.
From the evil one protect me.
At the hour of me death call me.
Into your presence lead me,
to praise you with all your saints
for ever and ever.
R. Amen.

## 22. PRAYER BEFORE A CRUCIFIX

Good and gentle Jesus,
I kneel before you.
I see and I ponder your five wounds.
My eyes behold what David prophesied about
　you:
"They have pierced my hands and feet;
they have counted all my bones."

Engrave on me this image of yourself.
Fulfill the yearnings of my heart:
give me faith, hope, and love,
repentance for my sins,
and true conversion of life.
R. Amen.

## 23. PANGE LINGUA

Hail our Savior's glorious Body,
Which his Virgin Mother bore;
Hail the Blood which, shed for sinners,
Did a broken world restore;
Hail the sacrament most holy,
Flesh and Blood of Christ adore!

Come, adore this wondrous presence;
Bow to Christ, the source of grace!
Here is kept the ancient promise
Of God's earthly dwelling-place!
Sight is blind before God's glory,
Faith alone may see his face!

Glory be to God the Father,
Praise to his coequal Son,
Adoration to the Spirit,
Bond of love, in Godhead one!
Blest be God by all creation
Joyously while ages run!

Thomas Aquinas<br>Trans. by James Quinn, SJ

# MARY, MOTHER OF GOD

From its first generations, the Church has invoked Mary in prayer. The first prayer given below dates from the third century; it is often called the "Sub tuum praesidium" from the first Latin words. The second became popular more than a thousand years later. Some of the other texts that are addressed to Mary in this book are the Hail Holy Queen (page 94) and the Litany of the Blessed Virgin Mary (page 343).

## 24. ANCIENT PRAYER TO THE VIRGIN

We turn to you for protection,
holy Mother of God.
Listen to our prayers
and help us in our needs.
Save us from every danger,
glorious and blessed Virgin.

## 25. MEMORARE

Remember, most loving Virgin Mary,
never was it heard
that anyone who turned to you for help
was left unaided.

Inspired by this confidence,
though burdened by my sins,
I run to your protection
for you are my mother.

Mother of the Word of God,
do not despise my words of pleading
but be merciful and hear my prayer.
R. Amen.

## 26. HAIL, MARY

Hail Mary, full of grace,
the Lord is with you!
Blessed are you among women,
and blessed is the fruit of your womb, Jesus.
Holy Mary, mother of God,
pray for us sinners,
now and at the hour of our death.
R. Amen.

## 27. THE ANGELUS

V. The angel spoke God's message to Mary,
R. and she conceived of the Holy Spirit.
Hail, Mary. . . .

V. "I am the lowly servant of the Lord:
R. let it be done to me according to your word."
Hail, Mary. . . .

V. And the Word became flesh
R. and lived among us.
Hail, Mary. . . .

V. Pray for us, holy Mother of God,
R. that we may become worthy of the promises
    of Christ.

Let us pray.

Lord,
fill our hearts with your grace:
once, through the message of an angel
you revealed to us the incarnation of your Son;
now, through his suffering and death
lead us to the glory of his resurrection.

We ask this through Christ our Lord.
R. Amen.


## 28. THE ROSARY

The rosary is another prayer that, in its repetition, draws us into contemplation of the mysteries of our salvation. The rosary begins with the Apostles' Creed (page 375), followed by the Lord's Prayer and three Hail Mary's. Each of five decades is made up of ten Hail Mary's, preceded by the Lord's Prayer and followed by the Glory to the Father. The rosary concludes with the "Hail, Holy Queen" (page 94). Each decade has traditionally been given to pondering one aspect of the paschal mystery. Most often, the rosary is prayed with beads that denote each prayer.

It is traditional to pray the five decades of one of the mysteries of the rosary. According to custom, the joyful mysteries are used on Mondays and Thursdays and on the Sundays of Advent; the sorrowful mysteries are used on Tuesdays and Fridays and on the Sundays of Lent; the glorious mysteries are used on Wednesdays and Saturdays and on the remaining Sundays of the year.

The Joyful Mysteries
1. The Annunciation (Luke 1:30-33)
2. The Visitation (Luke 1:50-53)
3. The Nativity (Luke 2:10-11
4. The Presentation (Luke 2:29-32)
5. The Finding of Jesus in the Temple (Luke 2:48-52)

The Sorrowful Mysteries
1. The Agony in the Garden (Matthew 26:38-39)
2. The Scourging at the Pillar (John 19:1)
3. The Crowning with Thorns (Mark 15:16-17)
4. The Carrying of the Cross (John 19:17)
5. The Crucifixion (John 19:28-30)

The Glorious Mysteries
1. The Resurrection (Mark 16:6-8)
2. The Ascension (Acts 1:10-11)
3. The Coming of the Holy Spirit (Acts 2:1-4)
4. The Assumption of Mary (Song of Songs 2:3-6)
5. The Coronation of Mary (Luke 1:51-54)

# INVOCATIONS

These short texts suggest another form of prayer: a phrase that is repeated slowly, over and over again.

## 29. INVOCATIONS

Father.

Jesus.

Praised be Jesus Christ.

Lord, I believe in you.

Lord, I adore you.

Lord, I hope in you.

Lord, I love you.

All for love of you.

Thanks be to God.

Let us bless the Lord.

Your kingdom come.

Your will be done.

As God wills.

Help me, O God.

Strengthen me, Lord.

Lord, hear me.

Lord, save me.

Lord, have mercy.

Lord, spare me.

Lord, do not abandon me.

Lord Jesus Christ, Son of the living God,
have mercy on me, a sinner.

Glory to God in the highest.

Lord, how great you are.

Praise the Lord!

Alleluia!

Amen.

Come, Lord Jesus!

Hail, Mary.

We adore you, O Christ, and we bless you:
because by your holy cross you have redeemed
the world.

Blessed be the Holy Trinity.

Christ is victor, Christ is ruler, Christ is Lord of all.

Heart of Jesus , burning with love for us, inflame our hearts with love for you.

Heart of Jesus, I trust in you.

Heart of Jesus, all for love of you.

Sacred Heart of Jesus, have mercy on us.

My God and my all.

O God, be merciful to me a sinner.

Luke 18:13

Let me praise you, Virgin most holy: give me strength against your enemies.

Teach me to do your will, for you are my God.

Psalm 143:10

Lord, increase our faith.

Luke 17:5

[Lord,] I do believe, help my unbelief!

Mark 9:24

Lord, make our minds one in truth and our hearts one in love.

Lord, save us! We are perishing.

Matthew 8:25

My Lord and my God!

John 20:28

Loving heart of Mary, be my refuge.

Glory to the Father, and to the Son,
and to the Holy Spirit:
as it was in the beginning, is now,
and will be for ever.
Amen.

Jesus, Mary, and Joseph.

Jesus, Mary, and Joseph, I give you my heart and
my soul.
Jesus, Mary, and Joseph, assist me in the hour of
my death.
Jesus, Mary, and Joseph, may I die and rest in
peace with you.

Jesus, gentle and humble of heart, make my
heart like yours.

Cf. Matthew 11:29

May the Blessed Sacrament be praised and
adored for ever.

Stay with us, Lord.

Mother of sorrows, pray for us.

My Mother, my hope.

Lord, send laborers into your harvest.

Cf. Matthew 9:38; Luke 10:2

All holy men and women, pray for us.

Pray for us, holy Mother of God,
that we may become worthy of the promises of
Christ.

Father, into your hands I commend my spirit.

Psalm 31:6; Luke 23:46

Lord Jesus, in your mercy grant them eternal
rest.

Queen conceived without original sin, pray for
us.

Holy Mother of God, ever Virgin Mary, intercede
for us.

Holy Mary, pray for us.

You are the Messiah, the Son of the living God.

Matthew 16:16

God is light, and in him there is no darkness.

1 John 1:5

God is love, and whoever remains in love
remains in God.

1 John 4:16

# BAPTISMAL PROMISES AND CREEDS

These texts are not prayers but statements of belief. The first two, which are forms of the renewal of the promises made at baptism, put into brief but strong language the Christian's rejection of evil in all its manifestations and acceptance of the path of life found in the Church. The two creeds that follow are summary statements of the mystery into which we are baptized. The Nicene Creed was composed in the fourth century. The Apostles' Creed took its present form in the eighth century.

## 30. RENUNCIATION OF SIN AND PROFESSION OF FAITH

V. Do you reject sin so as to live in the freedom of God's children?

R. I do.

V. Do you reject the glamor of evil and refuse to be mastered by sin?

R. I do.

V. Do you reject Satan, father of sin and prince of darkness?

R. I do.

V. Do you believe in God, the Father almighty, creator of heaven and earth?

R. I do.

V. Do you believe in Jesus Christ, his only Son our Lord, who was born of the Virgin Mary, was crucified, died, and was buried, rose from the dead, and is now seated at the right hand of the Father?
R. I do.

V. Do you believe in the Holy Spirit, the holy catholic Church, the communion of saints, the forgiveness of sins, the resurrection of the body, and life everlasting?
R. I do.

V. This is our faith. This is the faith of the Church. We are proud to profess it in Christ Jesus our Lord.
R. Amen.

## 31. THE RENEWAL OF BAPTISMAL VOWS

V. Do you reaffirm your renunciation of evil and renew your commitment to Jesus Christ?
R. I do.

V. Do you believe in God the Father?
R. I believe in God, the Father almighty, creator of heaven and earth.

V. Do you believe in Jesus Christ, the Son of God?
R. I believe in Jesus Christ, his only Son, our Lord.
He was conceived by the power of the Holy Spirit and born of the Virgin Mary.

He suffered under Pontius Pilate, was
  crucified, died, and was buried.
He descended to the dead.
On the third day he rose again.
He ascended into heaven, and is seated
  at the right hand of the Father.
He will come again to judge the living and the
  dead.

V. Do you believe in the Holy Spirit?
R. I believe in the Holy Spirit,
  the holy catholic Church,
  the communion of saints,
  the forgiveness of sins,
  the resurrection of the body,
  and the life everlasting.

V. Will you continue in the apostles' teaching
  and fellowship,
  in the breaking of bread, and in the prayers?
R. I will, with God's help.

V. Will you persevere in resisting evil,
  and, whenever you fall into sin,
  repent and return to the Lord?
R. I will, with God's help.

V. Will you proclaim by word and example
  the Good News of God in Christ?
R. I will, with God's help.

V. Will you seek and serve Christ in all persons,
  loving your neighbor as yourself?
R. I will, with God's help.

V. Will you strive for justice and peace among all
people,
and respect the dignity of every human
being?
R. I will, with God's help.

May Almighty God,
the Father of our Lord Jesus Christ,
who has given us a new birth by water and the
Holy Spirit,
and bestowed upon us the forgiveness of sins,
keep us in eternal life by his grace,
in Christ Jesus our Lord.
R. Amen.


## 32. NICENE CREED

We believe in one God,
the Father, the Almighty,
maker of heaven and earth,
of all that is seen and unseen.

We believe in one Lord, Jesus Christ,
the only Son of God,
eternally begotten of the Father,
God from God, Light from Light,
true God from true God,
begotten, not made, one in Being with the
Father.
Through him all things were made.
For us men and for our salvation
he came down from heaven:
by the power of the Holy Spirit
he was born of the Virgin Mary, and
became man.

For our sake he was crucified under Pontius
Pilate;
he suffered, died, and was buried.
On the third day he rose again
in fulfillment of the Scriptures;
he ascended into heaven
and is seated at the right hand of the
Father.
He will come again in glory to judge the
living
and the dead, and his kingdom will have
no end.

We believe in the Holy Spirit, the Lord, the giver
of life,
who proceeds from the Father and the Son.
With the Father and the Son he is worshiped
and glorified.
He has spoken through the Prophets.
We believe in one holy catholic and apostolic
Church.
We acknowledge one baptism for the
forgiveness of sins.
We look for the resurrection of the dead,
and the life of the world to come.
Amen.

## 33. APOSTLES' CREED

I believe in God, the Father almighty,
creator of heaven and earth.
I believe in Jesus Christ, his only Son, our Lord.
He was conceived by the power of the
Holy Spirit
and born of the Virgin Mary.

He suffered under Pontius Pilate,
   was crucified, died, and was buried.
He descended to the dead.
On the third day he rose again.
He ascended into heaven,
   and is seated at the right hand of the Father.
He will come again to judge the living and the
   dead.

I believe in the Holy Spirit,
   the holy catholic Church,
   the communion of saints,
   the forgiveness of sins,
   the resurrection of the body,
   and the life everlasting.
Amen.

# IN OTHER LANGUAGES

The Scriptures that Jesus and his disciples knew were written in Hebrew. The spoken language of that time was Aramaic, another Semitic language. Greek became a common language of Christians as Paul and others preached the gospel to non-Jews. The gospels and letters of the New Testament were written in Greek. Latin, the language of the common people in Rome, gradually took the place of Greek for the Western Church. While the Scriptures and liturgies of the Church are now read and celebrated in hundreds of languages, some words and phrases from these beginnings remain as a witness to our history, to put into our lips some of the same words spoken by our ancestors.

**Alleluia.**

From the Hebrew for "Praise the Lord!" Saint Augustine wrote, "Here we chant in hope, there, in possession; here it is Alleluia *en route*, there it is Alleluia on arriving home." Jewish and Christian liturgies make use of the alleluia as an acclamation. In the West, Christians do not use this acclamation during Lent.

**Amen.**

A Hebrew word meaning "It is true!" or "So be it!" Revelation 3:14 makes "Amen" a title of Christ. With this acclamation, Jews and Christians commit themselves to what has been spoken in prayer.

**Marana tha.**

A grouping of Aramaic words meaning "Come, our Lord" or "Our Lord has come." It is found in 1 Corinthians 16:22. A similar form, "Come, Lord Jesus," is found in Revelation 22:20.

**Hosanna.**

An expression that, in its Hebrew origin, was an acclamation praying for safety or salvation. It has been used in both Jewish and Christian liturgy.

**Kyrie eleison.**

A Greek prayer that is translated, "Lord, have mercy." This litany response was retained in Greek even after the liturgy of the Western Churches came to be celebrated in Latin. As an acclamation of God's mercy, it is a word of joy and praise.

**Deo gratias.**

A Latin prayer or response meaning "Thanks be to God."

**Adoramus te, Christe.**

Latin for "We adore you, Christ." A similar prayer, *"Adoramus te, Domine,"* means "We adore you, Lord."

**Veni, Sancte Spiritus.**

Latin for "Come, Holy Spirit." These are the first words of the sequence (a special hymn before the gospel) sung on Pentecost (page 157).

**Gloria in excelsis Deo.**

The first Latin words of the hymn sung by the angels in Luke 2:14. The *New American Bible* translates this phrase, "Glory to God in the highest." In a longer form, the Gloria became a morning prayer of Christians (see page 26) and today is often part of the introductory rites at Sunday Mass.

**Sanctus.**

The Latin word that is translated "holy." It is the usual name of the acclamatory song at the beginning of the eucharistic prayer: "Holy, holy, holy Lord, God of power and might. . . ." The Greek word for "holy," *hagios,* long retained a place in the Roman liturgy of Good Friday. In the Hebrew Scriptures, the word *kadosh* (especially in Isaiah 6:3) is the sanctification of God's name. As such, the word maintains a vital role in Jewish liturgy.

## Agnus Dei.

The beginning of the Latin litany sung during the breaking of the bread at Mass and which means "Lamb of God." It is a reference to Christ, seen as an image of innocence associated with the story of deliverance from servitude (Exodus 12:1-13) and with Isaiah's poems of a suffering servant ("Like a lamb led to the slaughter. . . ." in Isaiah 53:7).

## Credo.

The first Latin word of the profession of faith, meaning "I believe" (page 375).

## Requiescat (requiescant) in pace.

A Latin prayer: "May he/she/they rest in peace." It is used in the Order of Christian Funerals.

## Pater Noster.

First Latin words of the Lord's Prayer. The entire Latin text is: *Pater noster, qui es in caelis: sanctificetur nomen tuum: adveniat regnum tuum: fiat voluntas tua, sicut in caelo et in terra. Panem nostrum cotidianum da nobis hodie; et dimitte nobis debita nostra, sicut et nos dimittimus debitoribus nostris; et ne nos inducas in tentationem; sed libera nos a malo. Amen.*

**Ave Maria.**

First Latin words of the Hail, Mary. The entire Latin text is: *Ave Maria, gratia plena, Dominus tecum, benedicta tu in mulieribus, et benedictus fructus ventris tui, Jesus. Sancta Maria, Mater Dei, ora pro nobis peccatoribus, nunc et in hora mortis nostrae. Amen.*

**Gloria Patri.**

First Latin words of the Glory to the Father. The entire Latin text is: *Gloria Patri et Filio et Spiritui Sancto: Sicut erat in principio, et nunc, et semper, et in saecula saeculorum. Amen.*

# MORNING PRAYER

The following is an example of Morning Prayer for Sunday as found in the Roman rite for the Liturgy of the Hours.

V. God, come to my assistance.
R. Lord, make haste to help me.

Glory to the Father, and to the Son,
    and to the Holy Spirit:
as it was the beginning, is now,
    and will be for ever.
Amen. Alleluia.

## HYMN

**(On Sundays)**

On this day, the first of days,
God the Father's name we praise;
Who, creation's Lord and spring,
Did the world from darkness bring.

On this day the eternal Son
Over death his triumph won;
On this day the Spirit came
With his gifts of living flame.

God, the blessed Three in One,
May thy holy will be done;
In thy word our souls are free.
And we rest this day with thee.

*On other days, "I Sing as I Arise Today," page 288, or another appropriate hymn may be sung.*

Psalmody

*Antiphon 1*   As morning breaks I look to you,
O God, to be my strength this day,
alleluia.

Psalm 63:2-9

O God, you are my God, for you I long;
for you my soul is thristing.
My body pines for you
like a dry, weary land without water.
So I gaze on you in the sanctuary
to see your strength and your glory.

For your love is better than life,
my lips will speak your praise.
So I will bless you all my life,
in your name I will lift up my hands.
My soul shall be filled as with a banquet,
my mouth shall praise you with joy.

On my bed I remember you.
On you I muse through the night
for you have been my help;
in the shadow of your wings I rejoice.
My soul clings to you;
your right hand holds me fast.

Glory to the Father, and to the Son,
   and to the Holy Spirit:
as it was the beginning, is now,
   and will be for ever.
Amen.

*Psalm-prayer*

Father, creator of unfailing light, give that same light to those who call to you. May our lips praise you; our lives proclaim your goodness; our work give you honor, and our voices celebrate you for ever.

*Antiphon 1*    As morning breaks I look to you, O God, to be my strength this day, alleluia.

*Antiphon 2*    From the midst of the flames the three young men cried out with one voice: Blessed be God, alleluia.

Daniel 3:57-88, 56

Bless the Lord, all you works of the Lord.
Praise and exalt him above all forever.
Angels of the Lord, bless the Lord.
You heavens, bless the Lord.
All you waters above the heavens, bless the Lord.
All you hosts of the Lord, bless the Lord.
Sun and moon, bless the Lord.
Stars of heaven, bless the Lord.

Every shower and dew, bless the Lord.
All you winds, bless the Lord.
Fire and heat, bless the Lord.
Cold and chill, bless the Lord.
Dew and rain, bless the Lord.
Frost and chill, bless the Lord.
Ice and snow, bless the Lord
Nights and days, bless the Lord.

Light and darkness, bless the Lord.
Lightnings and clouds, bless the Lord.

Let the earth bless the Lord.
Praise and exalt him above all forever.
Mountains and hills, bless the Lord.
Everything growing from the earth, bless the
    Lord.
You springs, bless the Lord.
Seas and rivers, bless the Lord.
You dolphins and all water creatures, bless the
    Lord.
All you birds of the air, bless the Lord.
All you beasts wild and tame, bless the Lord.
You sons of men, bless the Lord.

O Israel, bless the Lord.
Praise and exalt him above all forever.
Priests of the Lord, bless the Lord.
Servants of the Lord, bless the Lord.
Spirits and souls of the just, bless the Lord.
Holy men of humble heart, bless the Lord
Hananiah, Azariah, Mishael, bless the Lord.
Praise and exalt him above all forever.

Let us bless the Father, and the Son, and the
    Holy Spirit.
Let us praise and exalt him above all forever.
Blessed are you, Lord, in the firmament of
    heaven.
Praiseworthy and glorious and exalted above all
    forever.

*Antiphon 2*   From the midst of the flames the
three young men cried out with one
voice: Blessed be God, alleluia.

*Antiphon 3*   Let the people of Zion rejoice in their
King, alleluia.

## Psalm 149

Sing a new song to the Lord,
his praise in the assembly of the faithful.
Let Israel rejoice in its maker,
let Zion's sons exult in their king.
Let them praise his name with dancing
and make music with timbrel and harp.

For the Lord takes delight in his people.
He crowns the poor with salvation.
Let the faithful rejoice in their glory,
shout for joy and take their rest.
Let the praise of God be on their lips
and a two-edged sword in their hand,

to deal out vengeance to the nations
and punishment on all the peoples;
to bind their kings in chains
and their nobles in fetters of iron;
to carry out the sentence pre-ordained;
this honor is for all his faithful.

Glory to the Father, and to the Son,
   and to the Holy Spirit:
as it was the beginning, is now,
   and will be for ever.
Amen.

*Psalm-prayer*

Let Israel rejoice in you, Lord, and acknowledge you as creator and redeemer. We put our trust in your faithfulness and proclaim the wonderful truths of salvation. May your loving kindness embrace us now and for ever.

*Antiphon 3*    Let the people of Zion rejoice in their King, alleluia.


**Reading**    Revelation 7:10,12

Salvation comes from our God, who is seated on the throne, and from the Lamb! Amen. Blessing and glory, wisdom and thanksgiving, honor, power, and might be to our God forever and ever. Amen.


**Silence**


**Response to the Word of God**

V.  Christ, Son of the living God, have mercy on us.
R.  Christ, Son of the living God, have mercy on us.

V.  You are seated at the right hand of the Father,
R.  have mercy on us.

V. Glory to the Father, and to the Son, and to the Holy Spirit.

R. Christ, Son of the living God, have mercy on us.

**Canticle of Zechariah**                  Luke 1:68-79

+ Blessed be the Lord, the God of Israel;
he has come to his people and set them free.

He has raised up for us a mighty savior,
born of the house of his servant David.

Through his holy prophets he promised of old
   that he would save us from our enemies,
   from the hands of all who hate us.

He promised to show mercy to our fathers
and to remember his holy covenant.

This was the oath he swore to our father
   Abraham:
to set us free from the hands of our enemies,
free to worship him without fear,
   holy and righteous in his sight all the days of our
   life.

You, my child, shall be called the prophet of the
   Most High;
for you will go before the Lord to prepare his
   way,
to give his people knowledge of salvation
by the forgiveness of their sins.

In the tender compassion of our God
the dawn from on high shall break upon us,
to shine on those who dwell in darkness and the
    shadow of death,
and to guide our feet into the way of peace.

Glory to the Father, and to the Son,
    and to the Holy Spirit:
as it was in the beginning, is now,
    and will be for ever.
Amen.


**Intercessions**

Christ is the sun that never sets, the true light
that shines on every person. Let us call out to
him in praise:

R. Lord, you are our life and our salvation.

Creator of the stars, we thank you for your gift,
the first rays of the dawn, and we commemorate
your resurrection. R.

May your Holy Spirit teach us to do your will
today, and may your Wisdom guide us always. R.

Each Sunday give us the joy of gathering as your
people, around the table of your word and your
body. R.

From our hearts we thank you, for your countless blessings. R.

Our Father. . . .

**Concluding Prayer** (The opening prayer from the Sunday Mass or the following prayer is then said.)

Father of love,
hear our prayers.
Help us to know your will
and to do it with courage and faith.

Grant this through our Lord Jesus Christ,
    your Son,
who lives and reigns with you and the
    Holy Spirit,
one God, for ever and ever.
R. Amen.

**Dismissal**

May the Lord bless us,
protect us from all evil
and bring us to everlasting life.
R. Amen.

# EVENING PRAYER

The following is an example of Evening Prayer (Vespers) for Sunday as found in the Roman rite for the Liturgy of the Hours.

V. God, come to my assistance.
R. Lord, make haste to help me.

Glory to the Father, and to the Son,
    and to the Holy Spirit:
As it was in the beginning, is now,
    and will be for ever.
Amen. Alleluia.

**Hymn** (for example: "O Radiant Light,"
        page 46).

**Psalmody**

*Antiphon 1*    Like burning incense, Lord, let my
                prayer rise up to you.

### Psalm 141

I have called to you, Lord; hasten to help me!
Hear my voice when I cry to you.
Let my prayer arise before you like incense,
the raising of my hands like an evening oblation.

Set, O Lord, a guard over my mouth;
keep watch, O Lord, at the door of my lips!
Do not turn my heart to things that are wrong,
to evil deeds with those who are sinners.

Never allow me to share in their feasting.
If the upright strike or reprove me it is kindness;
but let the oil of the wicked not anoint my head.
Let my prayer be ever against their malice.

Their leaders were thrown down by the side of
    the rock;
then they understood that my words were kind.
As a millstone is shattered to pieces on the
    ground,
so their bones were strewn at the mouth of the
    grave.

To you, Lord God, my eyes are turned;
in you I take refuge; spare my soul!
From the trap they have laid for me keep me
    safe;
keep me from the snares of those who do evil.

Let the wicked fall into the traps they have set
whilst I pursue my way unharmed.


*Psalm-prayer*

Lord, from the rising of the sun to its setting
your name is worthy of all praise. Let our prayer
come like incense before you. May the lifting up
of our hands be as an evening sacrifice acceptable
to you, Lord our God.

*Antiphon 1*  Like burning incense, Lord, let my
prayer rise up to you.

*Antiphon 2*  You are my refuge, Lord; you are all
that I desire in life.

## Psalm 142

With all my voice I cry to the Lord,
with all my voice I entreat the Lord.
I pour out my trouble before you;
I tell you all my distress
while my spirit faints within me.
But you, O Lord, know my path.

On the way where I shall walk
they have hidden a snare to entrap me.
Look on my right and see:
there is not one who takes my part.
I have no means of escape,
not one who cares for my soul.

I cry to you, O Lord.
I have said: "You are my refuge,
all I have left in the land of the living."
Listen then to my cry
for I am in the depths of distress.

Rescue me from those who pursue me
for they are stronger than I.
Bring my soul out of this prison
and then I shall praise your name.
Around me the just will assemble
because of your goodness to me.

Glory to the Father, and to the Son,
   and to the Holy Spirit:
as it was the beginning, is now,
   and will be for ever.
Amen.


*Psalm-prayer*

Lord, we humbly ask for your goodness. May
you help us to hope in you, and give us a share
with your chosen ones in the land of the living.

*Antiphon 2*   You are my refuge, Lord; you are all
that I desire in life.

*Antiphon 3*   The Lord Jesus humbled himself,
and God exalted him for ever.


**Canticle**                                   Philippians 2:6-11

+ Though he was in the form of God,
Jesus did not deem equality with God
something to be grasped at.

Rather, he emptied himself
and took the form of a slave,
being born in the likeness of men.

He was known to be of human estate,
and it was thus that he humbled himself,
obediently accepting even death,
death on a cross!

Because of this,
God highly exalted him
and bestowed on him the name
above every other name,

so that at Jesus' name
every knee must bend
in the heavens, on the earth,
and under the earth,
and every tongue proclaim
to the glory of God the Father:
JESUS CHRIST IS LORD!

## Reading      Romans 11:33-36

Oh, the depth of the riches and wisdom and
knowledge of God! How inscrutable are his
judgments and how unsearchable his ways!
   "For who has known the mind of the Lord
      or who has been his counselor?"
   "Or who has given him anything
      that he may be repaid?"
For from him and through him and for him are
all things. To him be glory forever. Amen.

## Silence

## Response to the Word of God

V. Our hearts are filled with wonder
   as we contemplate your works, O Lord.
R. Our hearts are filled with wonder
   as we contemplate your works, O Lord.

V. We praise the wisdom which wrought them all,
R. as we contemplate your works, O Lord.

V. Glory to the Father, and to the Son, and to the Holy Spirit:
R. Our hearts are filled with wonder as we contemplate your works, O Lord.

**Canticle of Mary**                    Luke 1:46-55

+ My soul proclaims the greatness of the Lord,
my spirit rejoices in God my Savior
for he has looked with favor on his lowly
    servant.

From this day all generations will call me blessed:
the Almighty has done great things for me,
and holy is his Name.

He has mercy on those who fear him
in every generation.

He has shown the strength of his arm,
he has scattered the proud in their conceit.

He has cast down the mighty from their thrones,
and has lifted up the lowly.

He has filled the hungry with good things,
and the rich he has sent away empty.

He has come to the help of his servant Israel
for he has remembered his promise of mercy,
the promise he made to our fathers,
to Abraham and his children for ever.

Glory to the Father,
    and to the Son, and to the Holy Spirit:
as it was in the beginning, is now,
    and will be for ever.
Amen.


**Intercessions**

We give glory to the one God—Father, Son, and
Holy Spirit—and in our weakness we pray:

R. Lord, be with your people.

Holy Lord, Father all-powerful, let justice spring
up on the earth then your people will dwell in
the beauty of peace. R.

Let every nation come into your kingdom, so that
all peoples will be saved. R.

Let married couples live in your peace, and grow
in mutual love. R.

Reward all who have done good to us, Lord, and
grant them eternal life. R.

Look with compassion on victims of hatred and
war, grant them heavenly peace. R.

Our Father. . . .

**Concluding Prayer** (The opening prayer from the Sunday Mass or the following prayer is then said.)

Lord,
guide the course of world events
and give your Church the joy and peace
of serving you in freedom.

We ask this through our Lord Jesus Christ,
    your Son,
who lives and reigns with you and the
    Holy Spirit,
one God, for ever and ever.
R. Amen.


**Dismissal**

May the Lord bless us,
protect us from all evil
and bring us to everlasting life.
R. Amen.

# APPENDIX

# CALENDAR

The Church's calendar of seasons was noted at the beginning of Part II (see page 99). Each year, the Church also marks the feasts of saints and various days that commemorate events in the life of Jesus. These days are assigned different designations, depending on their importance. Those of greatest significance are called "solemnities" (**BOLD CAPITAL LETTERS** in the calendar below); next are "feasts" (**bold type**); then "memorials" (Roman type); and finally "optional memorials" (*italic*).

The calendar that follows combines the general calendar of the universal Church with the particular calendar of the dioceses of the United States. Many saints not listed here have days of remembrance in the particular calendars of other countries, dioceses, or regions. A complete list of all the saints of the Church and the dates of their deaths is found in the *Roman Martyrology*.

Families often celebrate the feasts of saints whose names are given to members of the family.

# JANUARY

| | | |
|---|---|---|
| 1 | **MARY, MOTHER OF GOD** | solemnity |
| 2 | Basil the Great and Gregory Nazianzen, bishops and doctors | memorial |
| 4 | Elizabeth Ann Seton, religious | memorial |
| 5 | John Neumann, bishop | memorial |
| 6 | *Blessed André Bessette, religious* | |
| 7 | *Raymond of Penyafort, priest* | |
| 13 | *Hilary, bishop and doctor* | |
| 17 | Anthony, abbot | memorial |
| 20 | *Fabian, pope and martyr Sebastian, martyr* | |
| 21 | Agnes, virgin and martyr | memorial |
| 22 | *Vincent, deacon and martyr* | |
| 24 | Francis de Sales, bishop and doctor | memorial |
| 25 | **Conversion of Paul, apostle** | feast |
| 26 | Timothy and Titus, bishops | memorial |

27   *Angela Merici, virgin*

28   Thomas Aquinas, priest
     and doctor                    memorial

31   John Bosco, priest           memorial

Sunday between January 2 and 8:
**EPIPHANY**                       solemnity

Sunday after Epiphany: **Baptism
of the Lord**                      feast


## FEBRUARY

2   **Presentation of the Lord**   feast

3   *Blase, bishop and martyr
    Ansgar, bishop*

5   Agatha, virgin and martyr      memorial

6   Paul Miki and companions,
    martyrs                        memorial

8   *Jerome Emiliani*

10  Scholastica, virgin            memorial

11  *Our Lady of Lourdes*

14  Cyril, monk, and Methodius,
    bishop                         memorial

## MARCH

# APRIL

| | | |
|---|---|---|
| 2 | *Francis of Paola, hermit* | |
| 4 | *Isidore, bishop and doctor* | |
| 5 | *Vincent Ferrer, priest* | |
| 7 | John Baptist de la Salle, priest | memorial |
| 11 | Stanislaus, bishop and martyr | memorial |
| 13 | *Martin I, pope and martyr* | |
| 21 | *Anselm, bishop and doctor* | |
| 23 | *George, martyr* | |
| 24 | *Fidelis of Sigmaringen, priest and martyr* | |
| 25 | **Mark, evangelist** | feast |
| 28 | *Peter Chanel, priest and martyr* | |
| 29 | Catherine of Siena, virgin and doctor | memorial |
| 30 | *Pius V, pope* | |

# MAY

1  *Joseph the Worker*

2  Athanasius, bishop and
   doctor                                     memorial

3  **Philip and James, apostles**      feast

12 *Nereus and Achilleus, martyrs*
   *Pancras, martyr*

14 **Matthias, apostle**                feast

15 *Isidore*

18 *John I, pope and martyr*

20 *Bernardine of Siena, priest*

25 *Venerable Bede, priest and*
   *doctor*
   *Gregory VII, pope*
   *Mary Magdalene de Pazzi,*
   *virgin*

26 Philip Neri, priest                 memorial

27 *Augustine of Canterbury,*
   *bishop*

31 **Visitation**                      feast

First Sunday after Pentecost:
**HOLY TRINITY**                       solemnity

Sunday after Holy Trinity: **THE BODY AND BLOOD OF CHRIST**   solemnity

Friday following Second Sunday after Pentecost: **SACRED HEART**   solemnity

Saturday following Second Sunday after Pentecost: *Immaculate Heart of Mary*

# JUNE

| | | |
|---|---|---|
| 1 | Justin, martyr | memorial |
| 2 | *Marcellinus and Peter, martyrs* | |
| 3 | Charles Lwanga and companions, martyrs | memorial |
| 5 | Boniface, bishop and martyr | memorial |
| 6 | *Norbert, bishop* | |
| 9 | *Ephrem, deacon and doctor* | |
| 11 | Barnabas, apostle | memorial |
| 13 | Anthony of Padua, priest and doctor | memorial |
| 19 | *Romuald, abbot* | |

| 21 | Aloysius Gonzaga, religious | memorial |
|----|----|----|
| 22 | *Paulinus of Nola, bishop*<br>*John Fisher, bishop and martyr,*<br>*and Thomas More, martyr* | |
| 24 | **BIRTH OF JOHN THE**<br>**BAPTIST** | solemnity |
| 27 | *Cyril of Alexandria, bishop*<br>*and doctor* | |
| 28 | Irenaeus, bishop and martyr | memorial |
| 29 | **PETER AND PAUL,**<br>**APOSTLES** | solemnity |
| 30 | *First Martyrs of the Church of*<br>*Rome* | |

## JULY

| 3 | **Thomas, apostle** | feast |
|----|----|----|
| 4 | *Elizabeth of Portugal* | |
| 5 | *Anthony Zaccaria, priest* | |
| 6 | *Maria Goretti, virgin and*<br>*martyr* | |
| 11 | Benedict, abbot | memorial |

| | | |
|---|---|---|
| 13 | *Henry* | |
| 14 | Blessed Kateri Tekakwitha, virgin | memorial |
| | *Camillus de Lellis, priest* | |
| 15 | Bonaventure, bishop and doctor | memorial |
| 16 | *Our Lady of Mount Carmel* | |
| 21 | *Lawrence of Brindisi, priest and doctor* | |
| 22 | Mary Magdalene | memorial |
| 23 | *Bridget, religious* | |
| 25 | **James, apostle** | feast |
| 26 | Joachim and Ann, parents of Mary | memorial |
| 29 | Martha | memorial |
| 30 | *Peter Chrysologus, bishop and doctor* | |
| 31 | Ignatius of Loyola, priest | memorial |

# AUGUST

| | | |
|---|---|---|
| 1 | Alphonsus Liguori, bishop and doctor | memorial |
| 2 | *Eusebius of Vercelli, bishop* | |
| 4 | John Vianney, priest | memorial |
| 5 | *Dedication of Saint Mary Major* | |
| 6 | **Transfiguration** | feast |
| 7 | *Sixtus II, pope and martyr, and companions, martyrs Cajetan, priest* | |
| 8 | Dominic, priest | memorial |
| 10 | **Lawrence, deacon and martyr** | feast |
| 11 | Clare, virgin | memorial |
| 13 | *Pontian, pope and martyr, and Hippolytus, priest and martyr* | |
| 14 | Maximilian Mary Kolbe, priest and martyr | memorial |
| 15 | **ASSUMPTION** | solemnity |
| 16 | *Stephen of Hungary* | |
| 19 | *John Eudes, priest* | |

| | | |
|---|---|---|
| 20 | Bernard, abbot and doctor | memorial |
| 21 | Pius X, pope | memorial |
| 22 | Queenship of Mary | memorial |
| 23 | *Rose of Lima, virgin* | |
| 24 | **Bartholomew, apostle** | feast |
| 25 | *Louis*<br>*Joseph Calasanz, priest* | |
| 27 | Monica | memorial |
| 28 | Augustine, bishop and doctor | memorial |
| 29 | Beheading of John the Baptist, martyr | memorial |

## SEPTEMBER

| | | |
|---|---|---|
| 3 | Gregory the Great, pope and doctor | memorial |
| 8 | **Birth of Mary** | feast |
| 9 | Peter Claver, priest | memorial |
| 13 | John Chrysostom, bishop and doctor | memorial |

| 14 | **Triumph of the Cross** | feast |
| 15 | Our Lady of Sorrows | memorial |
| 16 | Cornelius, pope and martyr, and Cyprian, bishop and martyr | memorial |
| 17 | *Robert Bellarmine, bishop and doctor* | |
| 19 | *Januarius, bishop and martyr* | |
| 20 | Andrew Kim Taegon, priest and martyr, Paul Chong Hasang and companions, martyrs | memorial |
| 21 | **Matthew, apostle and evangelist** | feast |
| 26 | *Cosmas and Damian, martyrs* | |
| 27 | Vincent de Paul, priest | memorial |
| 28 | *Wenceslaus, martyr* *Lawrence Ruiz and companions, martyrs* | |
| 29 | **Michael, Gabriel, and Raphael, archangels** | feast |
| 30 | Jerome, priest and doctor | memorial |

# OCTOBER

| | | |
|---|---|---|
| 1 | Theresa of the Child Jesus, virgin | memorial |
| 2 | Guardian Angels | memorial |
| 4 | Francis of Assisi | memorial |
| 6 | *Bruno, priest*<br>*Blessed Marie-Rose Durocher, virgin* | |
| 7 | Our Lady of the Rosary | memorial |
| 9 | *Denis, bishop and martyr, and companions, martyrs*<br>*John Leonardi, priest* | |
| 14 | *Callistus I, pope and martyr* | |
| 15 | Teresa of Jesus, virgin and doctor | memorial |
| 16 | *Hedwig, religious*<br>*Margaret Mary Alacoque, virgin* | |
| 17 | Ignatius of Antioch, bishop and martyr | memorial |
| 18 | **Luke, evangelist** | feast |

| 19 | Isaac Jogues and John de Brébeuf, priests and martyrs, and companions, martyrs | memorial |
|----|----|----|
| | *Paul of the Cross* | |
| 23 | *John of Capistrano, priest* | |
| 24 | *Anthony Claret, bishop* | |
| 28 | **Simon and Jude, apostles** | feast |

## NOVEMBER

| 1 | **ALL SAINTS** | solemnity |
|----|----|----|
| 2 | **ALL SOULS** | |
| 3 | *Martin de Porres, religious* | |
| 4 | Charles Borromeo, bishop | memorial |
| 9 | **Dedication of St. John Lateran** | feast |
| 10 | Leo the Great, pope and doctor | memorial |
| 11 | Martin of Tours, bishop | memorial |
| 12 | Josaphat, bishop and martyr | memorial |

| 13 | Frances Xavier Cabrini, virgin | memorial |
|----|-------------------------------|----------|
| 15 | *Albert the Great, bishop and doctor* | |
| 16 | *Margaret of Scotland* *Gertrude, virgin* | |
| 17 | Elizabeth of Hungary, religious | memorial |
| 18 | Philippine Duchesne, virgin | memorial |
| | *Dedication of the churches of Peter and Paul, apostles* | |
| 21 | Presentation of Mary | memorial |
| 22 | Cecilia, virgin and martyr | memorial |
| 23 | *Clement I, pope and martyr* *Columban, abbot* | |
| 30 | **Andrew, apostle** | feast |

Last Sunday in Ordinary Time:
**CHRIST THE KING**                    solemnity

## DECEMBER

| 3 | Francis Xavier, priest | memorial |
|---|------------------------|----------|

| 4 | *John Damascene, priest and doctor* | |
|---|---|---|
| 6 | *Nicholas, bishop* | |
| 7 | Ambrose, bishop and doctor | memorial |
| 8 | **IMMACULATE CONCEPTION** | solemnity |
| 11 | *Damasus I, pope* | |
| 12 | **Our Lady of Guadalupe** | feast |
| 13 | Lucy, virgin and martyr | memorial |
| 14 | John of the Cross, priest and doctor | memorial |
| 21 | *Peter Canisius, priest and doctor* | |
| 23 | *John of Kanty, priest* | |
| 25 | **CHRISTMAS** | solemnity |
| 26 | **Stephen, first martyr** | feast |
| 27 | **John, apostle and evangelist** | feast |
| 28 | **Holy Innocents, martyrs** | feast |
| 29 | *Thomas Becket, bishop and martyr* | |
| 31 | *Sylvester I, pope* | |

Sunday within the octave of
Christmas or, if there is no
Sunday within the octave,
December 30: **Holy Family**          feast

# ACKNOWLEDGMENTS

**Augsburg Publishing House/Fortress Press**
426 South Fifth Street, Box 1209, Minneapolis MN
55440

"Blessed are you, Lord of heaven and earth, for
you give . . ." (p. 300)
  Excerpt from *Occasional Services*, copyright ©
  1982. Reprinted by permission.

"Blessed are you, Lord of heaven and earth. You
formed . . ." (p. 300)
  Excerpt from *Occasional Services*, copyright ©
  1982. Reprinted by permission.

"God of compassion and grace . . ." (p. 313)
  Excerpt from *Occasional Services*, copyright ©
  1982. Reprinted by permission.

"O God, give your blessing to all who share this
room . . ." (p. 299)
  Excerpt from *Occasional Services*, copyright ©
  1982. Reprinted by permission.

"O God, protect our going out and our coming
in . . ." (p. 299)
  Excerpt from *Occasional Services*, copyright ©
  1982. Reprinted by permission.

"O God, the Lord of all . . ." (p. 314)
  Excerpt from *Occasional Services*, copyright ©
  1982. Reprinted by permission.

"O God, you fill the hungry with good things . . ." (p. 299)
> Excerpt from *Occasional Services*, copyright © 1982. Reprinted by permission.

"O God, you have bound us together in a common life . . ." (p. 314)
> Excerpt from *Occasional Services*, copyright © 1982. Reprinted by permission.

"Protect us, Lord, as we stay awake . . ." (p. 300)
> Excerpt from *Occasional Services*, copyright © 1982. Reprinted by permission.

**Geoffrey Chapman/Cassell Publishers Limited**
Artillery House, Artillery Row, London SW1P 1RT, England

"Hail our Saviour's glorious Body . . ." (p. 360)
> *Pange Lingua* translated by James Quinn, SJ, copyright © 1969. Reprinted by permission.

**The Church Hymnal Corporation**
800 Second Avenue, New York NY 10017

"As grain once scattered on the hillside . . ." (p. 60)
> Excerpt from "Father, We Thank Thee" by F. Bland Tucker in *The Hymnal 1982*, copyright © Church Pension Fund. Used by permission.

"God our creator, we are the work of your hands . . ." (p. 200)
> Excerpt from *Book of Common Prayer*, copyright © Church Pension Fund. Used by permission.

"God, we pray for our young people . . ." (p. 235)
Excerpt from *Book of Common Prayer*, copyright © Church Pension Fund. Used by permission.

"Kind Maker of the world, o hear . . ." (p. 319)
Translation of hymn of Gregory the Great in *The Hymnal 1982*, copyright © Church Pension Fund. Used by permission.

"The Renewal of Baptismal Vows" (p. 372)
From *Book of Common Prayer*, copyright © Church Pension Fund. Used by permission.

**Concordia Publishing House**
3558 South Jefferson Avenue, Saint Louis MO 63118

"Thy strong word did cleave the darkness . . ." (p. 164)
Text by Martin Franzmann, copyright © 1969. Reprinted by permission.

**Harper & Row Publishers, Inc.**
10 East Fifty-Third Street, New York NY 10022

"Blessed are you, Lord our God, for you lead us . . ." (p. 290)
Excerpt from *Book of Family Prayer* by Gabe Huck, copyright © 1979 by The Seabury Press, Inc. Reprinted by permission of Harper & Row Publishers, Inc.

"For those who suffer most from war . . ." (p. 198)

Excerpt from *The Wideness of God's Mercy*, Vol. II, copyright © The Seabury Press, Inc. Reprinted by permission of Harper & Row Publishers, Inc.

"God, our refuge, our home is ever with you . . ." (p. 296)

Excerpt from *Book of Family Prayer* by Gabe Huck, copyright © 1979 by The Seabury Press, Inc. Reprinted by permission of Harper & Row Publishers, Inc.

"Loving God, your love for us is like that of a mother . . ." (p. 223)

Excerpt from *Book of Family Prayer* by Gabe Huck, copyright © 1979 by The Seabury Press, Inc. Reprinted by permission of Harper & Row Publishers, Inc.

"O God, you led your servant Abraham . . ." (p. 293)

Excerpt from *Book of Family Prayer* by Gabe Huck, copyright © 1979 by The Seabury Press, Inc. Reprinted by permission of Harper & Row Publishers, Inc.

"That the rights and needs of all may be recognized . . ." (p. 172)

Excerpt from *The Wideness of God's Mercy*, Vol. II, copyright © The Seabury Press, Inc. Reprinted by permission of Harper & Row Publishers, Inc.

## Hope Publishing Company
380 South Main Place, Carol Stream IL 60188

"For the fruits of this creation . . ." (p. 173)
Excerpts from *For the Fruits of His Creation* by F. Pratt Green, copyright © 1970. Used by permission. All rights reserved.

## The Liturgical Conference
810 Rhode Island Avenue, N.E., Washington DC 20017

"Exalted, compassionate God, grant perfect peace . . ." (p. 191)
Prayer for *Yom HaShoah*, copyright © The Liturgical Conference. Used by permission.

"Lord our God, see how oppression and violence . . ." (p. 195)
Prayer for *Martin Luther King's Birthday*, copyright © The Liturgical Conference. Used by permission.

## The Liturgical Press
St. John's Abbey, Collegeville MN 56321

"How splendid the cross of Christ! It brings life . . ." (p. 146)
Excerpt from *Springtime of the Liturgy* by Lucien Deiss (trans.), copyright © 1979, the Order of St. Benedict, Inc. Used by permission.

"What did you say then, each of you . . ." (p. 151)
Excerpt from *Springtime of the Liturgy* by Lucien Deiss (trans.), copyright © 1979, the Order of St. Benedict, Inc. Used by permission.

**Liturgy Training Publications**
1800 North Hermitage Avenue, Chicago IL
60622-1101

"All praise be yours, God our Creator . . ." (p. 63)
*Prayer for Fridays*, copyright © 1983, the Archdiocese of Chicago. Used by permission.

"Dear brothers and sisters, the glory of the Lord . . ." (pp. 102-103)
*Epiphany Proclamation* from the Italian Sacramentary. Translation by Peter Scagnelli, copyright © 1986, the Archdiocese of Chicago. Used by permission.

**Oxford University Press**
Walton Street, Oxford OX2 6DP, England

"God be in my head, and in my understanding . . ." (p. 35)
Excerpt from *The Oxford Book of Prayer*, copyright © 1985. Used by permission.

"Lord God, you made us out of nothing . . ." (pp. 223-224)
Excerpt from *The Oxford Book of Prayer*, copyright © 1985. Used by permission.

"O God, make the door of this house wide . . ." (p. 155)
Excerpt from *The Oxford Book of Prayer*, copyright © 1985. Used by permission.

"O God, we are conscious that many centuries of blindness . . ." (p. 191)
Excerpt from *The Oxford Book of Prayer*, copyright © 1985. Used by permission.

"We beg you, Lord to help and defend us . . ."
(p. 327)
> Excerpt from *The Oxford Book of Prayer*, copyright © 1985. Used by permission.

**Regnery Gateway, Inc.**
1130 17th Street, N.W., Suite 620, Washington DC 20036

"Night devoid of all dark . . ." (p. 149)
> Excerpt from *Early Christian Prayer*, translation of prayer by Asterius of Amasia, copyright © Regnery Gateway, Inc. Used by permission.

**Reverend Peter J. Scagnelli, Translator**
Holy Trinity Rectory, 134 Fuller Avenue, Central Falls RI 02863

"Again we keep this solemn fast . . ." (p. 136)
> Translation and copyright © by Peter J. Scagnelli. Used by permission.

"Holy Spirit, Lord Divine . . ." (p. 158)
> Translation and copyright © by Peter J. Scagnelli. Used by permission.

"O Sun of justice, Jesus Christ . . ." (p. 142)
> Translation and copyright © by Peter J. Scagnelli. Used by permission.

**Scottish Academic Press Limited**
33 Montgomery Street, Edinburgh EH7 5JX, Scotland

"Blessed are you, Lord, God of all creation . . ."
(p. 28)
> Excerpt from *Carmina Gadelica*, Vol. I, by Alexander Carmichael. Copyright © Scottish Academic Press Limited. Used by permission.

"Christ is shepherd over you . . ." (p. 95)
Excerpt from *Carmina Gadelica,* Vol. I, by
Alexander Carmichael. Copyright © Scottish
Academic Press Limited. Used by permission.

**William G. Storey, Translator**
Dept. of Theology, University of Notre Dame du
Lac, Notre Dame IN 46556

"For an evening that is perfect, holy, peace-
ful . . ." (pp. 328-329)
*Ancient Byzantine Litany* in *Morning Praise and
Evensong,* translation and copyright © by
William G. Storey. Used by permission.

"For the peace of the world, that a spirit of
respect . . ." (pp. 329-330)
*Ancient Byzantine Litany* in *Morning Praise and
Evensong,* translation and copyright © by
William G. Storey. Used by permission.

"O radiant Light, O Sun divine . . ." (pp. 46-47)
*"Phos Hilaron"* in *Morning Praise and Evensong,*
translation and copyright © by William G.
Storey. Used by permission.

**A. P. Watt, Limited**
20 John Street, London WC1P 2DL, England

"Bless the Lord, all you works of the Lord . . ."
(pp. 384-385)
Excerpt from the *Grail Psalms.* Used by permission of A.P. Watt, Ltd., on behalf of The
Grail, England.

"I have called you, Lord; hasten to help me . . ."
(pp. 391-392)
Excerpt from the *Grail Psalms*. Used by permission of A.P. Watt, Ltd., on behalf of The Grail, England.

"May the Lord bless us . . ." (p. 390)
Excerpt from the *Grail Psalms*. Used by permission of A.P. Watt, Ltd., on behalf of The Grail, England.

"O God, you are my God, for you I long . . ."
(p. 383)
Excerpt from the *Grail Psalms*. Used by permission of A.P. Watt, Ltd., on behalf of The Grail, England.

"Sing a new song to the Lord . . ." (p. 386)
Excerpt from the *Grail Psalms*. Used by permission of A.P. Watt, Ltd., on behalf of The Grail, England.

"We shall go up with joy . . ." (p. 106)
Excerpt from the *Grail Psalms*. Used by permission of A.P. Watt, Ltd., on behalf of The Grail, England.

"With all my voice I cry to the Lord . . ." (p. 393)
Excerpt from the *Grail Psalms*. Used by permission of A.P. Watt, Ltd., on behalf of The Grail, England.

# INDEX

Creeds, 371: Apostles Creed, 375; Nicene
Creed, 374
Crucifix, Prayer before a Crucifix, 360
Cyril, Saint (Cyril of Jerusalem), 151

Daughter, Blessing before Marriage, 240
Death: Gathering in the Presence of the Body,
273; Prayers after Death, 272; Prayers at the
Time of Death, 267; Prayers with the Dying,
269
*Deo Gratias*, 378
Devotion, Blessing of Objects of Devotion, 308
*Didache*, 60
Divine Praises, 334
Dressing, 28
Drink and Food, 40, 152

Easter (Paschaltime): At Table, 84; Blessing of
Easter Foods, 152; Easter Sunday, 151; Easter
Vigil, 149; Washing and Dressing, 29
Elderly, Communion of the Elderly, 256
Ember Days, 186, 192
Employment, Leaving for Employment, 292
Engaged Couples, Blessing of an Engaged
Couple, 236
Entertainment, Blessing of Objects for Use or
Entertainment, 307
Epiphany, Blessing of the Home and
Household, 126
Eucharist, Holy Eucharist, 359
Evening Intercessions and Prayer, 328, 391
*Exsultet*, 150
Eyes, When Opening the Eyes, 26

Factory (workplace), 304
Faith, Profession of Faith, 371
Family, Blessings of Family Members, 203
Fasting, 137, 159
Father's Day, 198
Feasts and Fasts, 159
Fields and Gardens, Blessing, 166
First Communion, Blessing before First
Communion, 231
Food and Drink, 40: Blessing of Easter Foods,
152; Mother's Blessing of a Child when
Nursing or Feeding, 226
Fourth of July (Independence Day), 199
Francis of Assisi, Saint, 124, 169, 174
Franzmann, Martin, 164

Fridays: Abstinence, 193; At Table on Fridays,
63; Good Friday, 145

Gardens and Fields, Blessing, 166
Gathering in the Presence of the Body, 273
Gathering to Meet, Prayer, 283
George Washington's Birthday, 196
*Gloria in excelsis Deo*, 26, 379
*Gloria Patri*, 25, 381
Glorious Mysteries of the Rosary, 365
Godparent's Blessing of a Child, 231
God's Will, Prayer in Times of Seeking God's
Will, 320
Going Out from Home Each Day, 32
Good Friday, 145
Graveside, Prayers at the Graveside, 280
Gravesites, visit to Gravesite, 178
Green, F. Pratt, 173
Gregory I, Saint, Pope (Gregory the Great),
136, 139
Guadalupe, Our Lady of Guadalupe, 185
Guests, Prayer for Welcoming Guests, 282

Hail Holy Queen (*Salve Regina*), 94
Hail, Mary, 37, 38, 90, 91, 363
Harvest, Assumption Day, 170
Holidays, National Days, 195
Holy Eucharist, 359
"Holy God, We Praise Thy Name," 333
Holy Innocents, Feast, 189
Holy Name of Jesus, Litany, 335
Holy Saturday, 147
Holy Thursday Evening, 144
Home: Blessing before Moving from a Home,
295; Blessing of the Home and Household,
126; Blessing on Bringing a Child into the
Home, 226; Blessing upon Moving into a
New Home, 297; Coming Home Each Day,
46; For the Day's Work at Home, 35; Going
Out from Home Each Day, 32; Leaving
Home, Blessing, 292; Placing of Palm
Branches in the Home, 140; Prayer for
Welcoming Guests, 282; Receiving Blessed
Candles at Home, 161
*Hosanna*, 378
Hours, *Liturgy of the Hours*, 331
Household, Blessing for a Household, 126, 206
Human Labor, Blessing for the Products of
Human Labor, 324